GREAT DECISIONS

JANUARY 2024

About the cover

The world's largest newly built container ship "Xinfu 103" completes outfitting at Yangzi Mitsui Shipyard in Taicang, in Suzhou, Jiangsu Province, China, March 19, 2023. It leaves its berth for a trial voyage at Zhoushan Sea. With a total length of 399.99 meters, a width of 61.3 meters and a maximum height of 78.1 meters above the keel, Xinfu 103 has a deck area of 24,000 square meters, equivalent to 3.3 standard football fields. The maximum number of container layers can reach 25, equivalent to the height of a 22-story building, and it can load 24,346 standard 20-foot containers at a time.

CFOTO/Future Publishing/Getty Images

FOREIGN POLICY ASSOCIATION 1918

GREAT DECISIONS IS A TRADEMARK OF THE FOREIGN POLICY ASSOCIATION.

© COPYRIGHT 2024 BY FOREIGN POLICY ASSOCIATION, INC., 551 FIFTH AVENUE, NEW YORK, NEW YORK 10176. All rights reserved.

No part of this book may be reproduced in any form, or by any means, without permission in writing from the publisher.

LIBRARY OF CONGRESS CONTROL NUMBER: 2022948788

ISBN: 978-0-87124-289-1

	Forward	3
1	The U.S. and the Middle East by Marc Lynch	5
2	Global trade and green energy by Bud Ward	17
3	Risky science across borders by Mila Rosenthal	28
4	Technology denial and Sino-American rivalry by Jonathan Chanis	38
5	Nato's future by Sarwar Kashmeri	49
6	Invisible Indonesia by Charles Sullivan	59
7	High Seas Treaty	71
8	Pandemic preparedness by Karen Jacobsen	81

WITHDRAWN

Researched as of November 10, 2023.
The authors are responsible for factual accuracy and for the views expressed.

FPA itself takes no position on issues of U.S. foreign policy.

Winnetka-Northfield Public Library District
Winnetka, IL 60093
(847) 446-7220

CHECK OUT
GREAT DECISIONS
HIGH SCHOOL

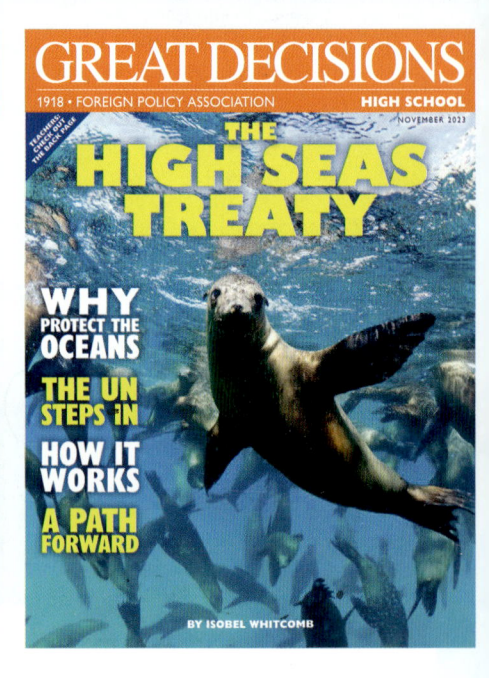

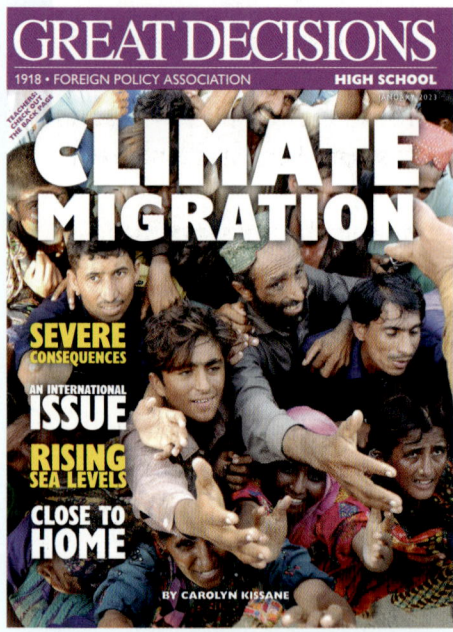

- **FREE monthly publication** highlighting some of the most important issues facing our world today
- Political cartoons, photos, and teen-focused reporting
- Discussion questions and debates encourage students to think critically about global issues
- Each issue highlights teens making a difference in the world and suggests ways for readers to make their own impact

Great Decisions: High School
Find all the publications for high school students on our website at www.fpa.org.

1918 • FOREIGN POLICY ASSOCIATION

GREAT DECISIONS

Editorial Advisory Committee

CHAIRMAN

David B.H. Denoon
*Professor of Politics and Economics
New York University*

Barbara Crossette
*Specialist on the UN
and South-Southeast Asia*

Michael Doyle
*Harold Brown Professor
of International Affairs,
Law and Political Science;
University Professor
Columbia University*

Christine E. Lucas
*Chief of Operations
Leadership Florida, Tallahassee*

Lawrence G. Potter
*Adjunct Associate Professor of
International and Public Affairs,
Columbia University*

Thomas G. Weiss
*Presidential Professor
of Political Science
The CUNY Graduate Center*

Karen M. Rohan
*FPA Editor in Chief
Ex officio*

Foreign Policy Association

Henry A. Fernandez
Chairman of the Board of Directors

Noel V. Lateef
President and CEO

EDITOR IN CHIEF
Karen M. Rohan

PHOTO EDITOR
Cynthia Carris Alonso

CONSULTING EDITOR
Kyle Piscioniere

MAPS AND CHARTS
Robert Cronan
Lucidity Information Design, LLC

Remarks by Noel V. Lateef, President and CEO, Foreign Policy Association, at World Affairs Councils of America National Conference in Washington, D.C., November 15, 2023

~~~~~~~~~~~

I am delighted to be here to recognize the World Affairs Council of Cincinnati and Northern Kentucky and the Cleveland Council on World Affairs as they cross their centennial threshold. I congratulate Michelle Harpenau Glandorf and Carina Van Vliet and their colleagues, their board of directors and members. Thank you for an extraordinary century of effort and success. Having celebrated the Foreign Policy Association's centenary five years ago, welcome to the centennial club.

Over the years, millions of Americans have participated in the programs offered by our network of 90 World Affairs Councils. These individuals have sought a more profound understanding of global challenges and the facts that must underpin effective policies. As a network, our common mission has been one of furtherance of access and transparency—a mission of imagination, voice and inclusion.

By bringing speakers, by engaging teachers and students, and through balanced, nonpartisan initiatives, such as FPA's Great Decisions national outreach program, we elevate public debates on pressing global issues, and thereby strengthen our democracy.

The purpose of bringing citizens together has not been to impose a particular view but rather to consider and weigh many views. I am reminded of the words of Bertrand Russell:

> *The world is suffering from intolerance and from the belief that vigorous action is admirable, even when misguided; whereas what is needed in our very complex, modern society is calm consideration, with readiness to call dogmas into question and freedom of mind to do justice to the most diverse points of view.*

I believe the Great Decisions outreach program offers a template for ventilating issues in a civil and constructive manner.

I find compelling the interest of Great Decisions discussion group participants in hearing what their peers have to say and to do so in an environment that is conducive to inquiry, as well as to advocacy.

In such a setting, the focus shifts from being better than someone else to attaining the best expression of one's self through study and critical thinking. This kind of ambience can and should be emulated on campuses today. I am pleased that many colleges and universities across the United States offer a Great Decisions course.

At the Foreign Policy Association, we have stressed the importance of engaging with higher education leaders across a broad spectrum. Our first Special Edition of Great Decisions, exploring the global ramifications of the Covid-19 pandemic, was a joint venture with the Hoover Institution at Stanford University. Our second Special Edition of Great Decisions, on the war in Ukraine and its impact on world order was a joint venture with the School of Public and International Affairs at Princeton University.

While we look back on a golden age at the Foreign Policy Association, we are not sitting on our laurels. Indeed as we strive in diverse ways to showcase the issues that matter, we are on the cusp of another golden age. With an inclusive approach, we find ourselves on the right side of history.

Our network, 90 World Affairs Councils strong, is positioned today, as never before, to truly make a difference in our democracy. In the words of Walt Whitman, "The strongest and sweetest songs yet remain to be sung."

Thank you, again, to the World Affairs Council of Cincinnati and Northern Kentucky and to the Cleveland Council on World Affairs for your dedication to the proposition that in a democracy the great decisions in international affairs are every citizen's concern; for all the hard work you put in over the last century. And now, on to the next.

Noel V. Lateef
President and Chief Executive Officer
Foreign Policy Association

1

The United States and the Middle East
by Marc Lynch

U.S. Secretary of State Antony Blinken disembarks from his plane in Amman during his visit to Jordan amid the ongoing conflict between Israel and the Palestinian Islamist group Hamas on November 3, 2023. JONATHAN ERNST/AFP/GETTY IMAGES

American hegemony has shaped the politics of the Middle East for many decades. But in recent years, that primacy has manifestly faded. Other great powers such as Russia and China have made significant inroads, while regional powers in the Middle East have demonstrated greater independence from America. Three successive American presidents, who in most ways could not be more different, have made clear in the aftermath of the disastrous occupation of Iraq their preference to reduce military commitments in the Middle East to focus on competition with China. But extracting the United States from the Middle East has proven difficult. The United States still has major interests in the region, including oil, Israel, and the challenge posed by Iran. Furthermore, reductions in America's role often leads to destabilizing, unintended consequences. And crises such as the October 2023 war between Israel and Hamas inevitably drag the United States back to active conflict mediation, regardless of its preferences.

This GREAT DECISIONS essay explains the history of America's role in the Middle East, discusses how conditions have changed in recent years, and then surveys the critical interests and issues in regional politics. Can the U.S. continue to defend its interests in the Middle East with a lower level of military and political involvement, or should it recommit to a leading role in regional order?

MARC LYNCH *is Professor of Political Science at The George Washington University, where he directs the Middle East Studies Program for the Elliott School of International Affairs. He is the director of the Project on Middle East Political Science, and editor of the book series* Columbia Studies in Middle East Politics. *His recent books include* The Arab Uprising: The Unfinished Revolutions of the New Middle East *and* The New Arab Wars: Anarchy and Uprisings in the Middle East.

1 The United States in the Middle East: A brief history

Iranian Prime Minister Mossadegh speaking forcefully to the crowd. He had just nationalized oil production and the last of the English had left the Abadan oil center on October 3, 1951. KEYSTONE-FRANCE/GETTY IMAGES

The deep entanglement between America and the Middle East is a fairly recent development. American domination of the Middle East is a distinctly post-World War II phenomenon. Prior to WWII, the U.S. was mostly an outsider; the European colonial powers dominated the Middle East. The Middle East, like much of the Global South, was shaped in those years by the competition between European imperial powers. France dominated North Africa, along with much of the rest of Francophone West Africa, and took power in Lebanon and Syria after World War I. Great Britain played a dominant role in Iran and controlled both Egypt and the coastal areas of the Arabian Peninsula, which were key transit points connecting it to colonial India. After World War I, London also assumed control over Palestine, Transjordan, and Iraq. Italy, in its quest to establish itself as a colonial power, did almost inconceivable damage to what would become Libya. It was the European powers, not the United States, that were the main target of the nationalist and anticolonial movements which swept the region after World War I.

That did not last. America's involvement in the Middle East escalated in tandem with the Cold War. Because of its oil reserves and central location, the Middle East quickly became a primary battlefield in the global struggle between the United States and the Soviet Union. By the Suez crisis of 1956, when the Eisenhower administration forced Britain and France to back down from their occupation of the Suez Canal, the U.S. had displaced the European powers in the Levant. France held power a bit longer in North Africa, but finally admitted defeat in the Algerian war for independence in 1962; Britain remained the primary power in the Gulf until 1971, when it officially ended its imperial role. In the place of the competition among multiple colonial powers that had structured the previous century, a bipolar division of global politics between the United States and the Soviet Union took hold in the Middle East. Middle Eastern regimes, many of them newly independent, were forced to choose sides in order to gain access to arms sales, economic support and political protection. These regimes proved to be masters at couching their local priorities in the language of socialism or anti-communism, while the superpowers worried that the loss of any local ally could set of a cascade of defections—the same "domino theory" that brought the United States into the Vietnam War.

For all the intense competition, regimes changed sides only rarely. The logic of bipolarity ensured that any country changing sides would have major implications for the perceived regional and global balance of power. There were a few major shifts. Iraq's 1958 revolution moved it from a British protectorate to an Arab nationalist regime that would soon gravitate toward Moscow. Iran's move toward an independent foreign policy under democratically elected Prime Minister Mossadegh, by contrast, was blocked in 1952 through a coup supported by Great Britain and the United States. In 1979, Egypt completed its transition from Soviet ally to American ally as part of its peace treaty with Israel, but in the same year the pro-American Shah of Iran was overthrown in the revolution that resulted in the creation of Ayatollah Khomeini's Islamic Republic of Iran. These epochal changes in regional order are the exceptions that demonstrate the rule: most regional states, most of the time, were locked into a global alliance structure.

Israel represented one of the key flashpoints in this Cold War competition. In both 1967 and 1973, wars between Israel and its Arab neighbors brought the United States and the Soviet Union as close to direct conflict as at any other point in the Cold War. Growing American support for Israel, particularly its airlift to resupply Israeli forces in the midst of the 1973 war, badly complicated its relations with its key Arab allies such as Saudi Ara-

! Before you read, download the companion **Glossary** that includes definitions, a guide to acronyms and abbreviations used in the article, and other material. Go to **www.fpa.org/great_decisions** and select a topic in the Resources section. (Top right)

THE U.S. AND THE MIDDLE EAST

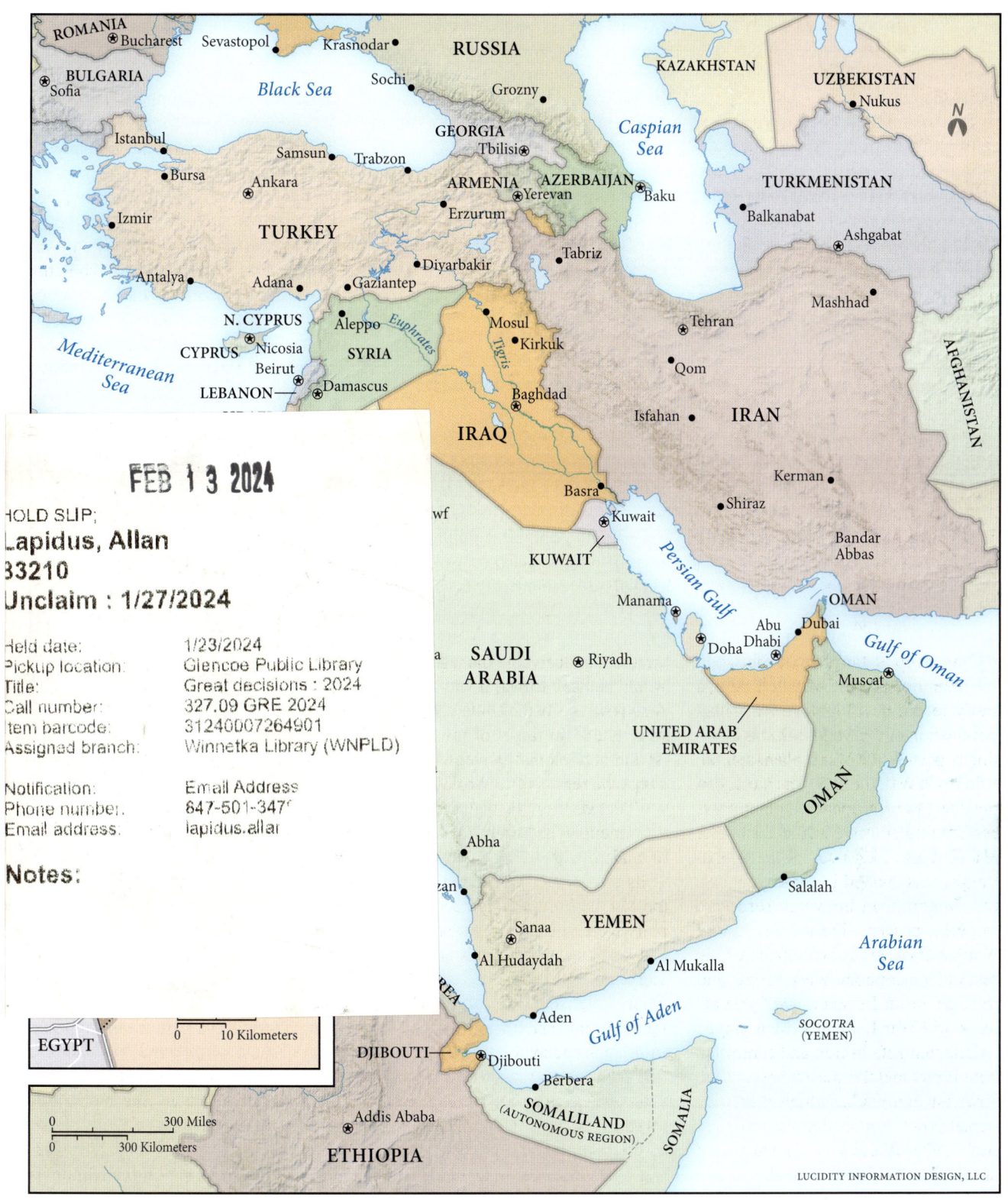

bia, which retaliated by installing the OPEC oil blockade. The United States used the shock waves of the 1973 war to take on a lead role in the peace negotiations following that war, seeking to exclude Moscow from the process while demonstrating to its estranged Arab allies that its mediation was the only way to force Israel to make concessions. The Camp David Accords, signed by Egypt and Israel in 1979, returned the captured Sinai peninsula to Egypt in exchange for peace and security guarantees, marking the culmination of that diplomacy and establishing Washington as a hegemonic power in the center of the Middle East—even as the Iranian revolution struck a major

7

blow to its position in the Gulf by turning its most powerful ally into a mortal enemy with revolutionary ambitions across the region.

The United States became increasingly involved militarily in the Gulf during the Iran-Iraq War (1980–88). It could hardly be indifferent to the largest conventional war in the region's modern history, even if the conflict involved Iraq (a long-time Soviet ally) and Iran (fiercely anti-American since the revolution). Nor was Washington prepared to move past the excruciating hostage crisis, which followed the 1979 seizure of the American Embassy in Tehran, or the new Islamic Republic's efforts to destabilize America's allies in the Gulf. The U.S. encouraged the creation of the Gulf Cooperation Council, bringing together the six oil-rich states of the Arabian Peninsula to pool their resources for protection against the two hostile warring powers. Rather cynically, the United States played both sides, secretly selling arms to Iran in exchange for the release of Hezbollah-held hostages in Lebanon, while simultaneously providing increasing amounts of aid to Iraq in the latter half of the decade. It only began to get directly involved, however, when the war began to affect oil shipping in the Gulf. In 1988, after the United States had reflagged Kuwaiti oil tankers as its own and then shot down an Iranian passenger jet, Iran finally agreed to a UN-mediated ceasefire agreement, ending the Middle East's longest conventional war. Iraq, even as it received increasing U.S. economic and military support, took advantage of the respite by carrying out a genocidal campaign against its Kurdish population in the north—a horrifying war crime that had little impact on Washington's efforts to woo it away from the Soviet Bloc.

The era of American primacy: From Bush to Clinton to Bush

The collapse of the Soviet Union and the end of the Cold War in 1989 set the stage for unprecedented American primacy in the region. It is important to understand that prior to 1990, the U.S. had no permanent military bases in the Middle East and only rarely sent its own forces to intervene; its role had always been offshore, working through local partners. When Saddam Hussein invaded Kuwait in the summer of 1990, he had good reason to believe that the United States would not intervene—an assumption that no Middle Eastern leader would make for decades to follow. After Iraq occupied Kuwait, the United States built an international coalition that would never have been possible during the Cold War and convinced a reluctant Saudi Arabia to host U.S. troops. The liberation of Kuwait involved a multinational coalition of more than half a million troops. It also laid the foundation for all the key pillars of U.S. policy during its decades of imperium in the region.

U.S. primacy was shaped by two key dimensions following the liberation of Kuwait. First, the Gulf War ended with Iraq's Saddam Hussein still in power, setting in motion a dozen years of episodic confrontations over arms inspections, justifying the imposition of some of the most draconian sanctions in human history, and leading the United States to leave a significant number of troops in bases around the Gulf. To this day, Iraqis keenly remember that the Bush administration called on them to rise up against Saddam in the chaotic endgame of the war, only to stand by and watch as Saddam's forces slaughtered those who did. Since the U.S. also still needed to defend its Gulf allies against Iran, the attempted "dual containment" of Iraq and Iran required American military presence, given the military weakness of the Gulf states.

Second, obtaining Arab support for the war against another Arab power required that Washington demonstrate willingness to find a solution to the Israeli-Palestinian conflict. After launching a grand regional peace process at Madrid in 1991, the U.S. oversaw nearly a decade of intense negotiations between Israel and the frontline Arab actors: Jordan, Syria, and the Palestinian Liberation Organization. Most other Arab states took part in multilateral negotiations over issues such as the environment, water, and economic development. This American-led peace process established the Palestinian Authority in Gaza and parts of the West Bank, but after seven difficult years, the talks ultimately failed to reach a final status agreement at Camp David in the final days of the Clinton administration. The peace process played a role, however, even if it failed to achieve peace: demonstrating effort allowed for the smoother functioning of an imperium based on both Israel and a range of Arab states that supported Palestinian claims.

(Original Caption) 10/22/1980-Basra, Iraq- Iraqi troops riding in Soviet-made tanks head for a pontoon bridge in an effort to cross the Karum River northeast of Khurramshahr. The smoke in the background is from the Abadan pipeline. Sporadic fighting continues along the southern front in a month-old Gulf war, with Iraqi forces racing to build a 60-mile highway across the desert from Basra to consolidate their seige of the Iranian city of Ahwaz. BETTMANN/GETTY IMAGES

THE U.S. AND THE MIDDLE EAST

The 1990s were the peak moment of America's Middle East, a decade in which the U.S. dominated political and security architecture in both the Levant (rooted in the Egypt-Israel Camp David peace agreement and the Israeli-Palestinian peace process) and the Gulf (built around military support to the Gulf Cooperation Council states and the containment of both Iraq and Iran). In those years, all roads led through Washington. But that very dominance sowed the seeds of instability to come. The sanctions on Iraq generated a humanitarian disaster that shocked the conscience of the world and became increasingly unsustainable, even as Saddam Hussein forced the end of the weapons inspections regime and rebuilt his domestic authority. The turbulent course of the Oslo process built enormous frustrations with the possibilities of Israeli-Palestinian peace, which would soon collapse into an exceptionally brutal war. And American dominance made it an attractive target for radical forces seeking to challenge the regional order—a challenge that would manifest in the terrorist attacks carried out by al-Qaeda on September 11, 2001.

The 2001 terrorist attacks led the U.S. to aggressively attempt to reshape the Middle East through the Global War on Terror, the invasion of Iraq, and a massively increased presence in the region. It is, perhaps, puzzling that the Bush administration attempted to radically transform a Middle Eastern order that had been built by the United States itself. For some in the administration, the shock of 9/11 had been so great that it forced a rethinking of all policy assumptions. For others, 9/11 opened an opportunity to pursue long-desired policies such as the overthrow of Saddam Hussein. Whatever the true reasons, Washington's new revisionist path upended regional politics with a whole range of unintended consequences.

Most significant was the invasion of Iraq and the disastrous occupation that followed. The overthrow of Saddam Hussein left the Iraqi state shattered, creating the conditions for a bloody sectarian civil war and a ruth-

U.S. Marine Major Bull Gurfein pulls down a poster of Iraqi President Saddam Hussein March 21, 2003, in Safwan, Iraq. Chaos reigned in southern Iraq as coalition troops continued their offensive to remove Iraq's leader from power. CHRIS HONDROS/GETTY IMAGES

lessly effective insurgency that killed millions of Iraqis and drove more than 10 million more into exile. The cost in American lives and treasure turned much of the American public against such Middle Eastern wars, with significant implications in the years to come. The war also dramatically empowered Iran by removing its primary military and political adversary, empowering its local Shi'a allies, and allowing Iran and its allies to claim the mantle of "resistance" to America's hegemonic order. In 2006, Iran's ally Hezbollah fought Israel to a stalemate, emerging as the political victor from the carnage of a war that Secretary of State Condoleezza Rice optimistically called "the birth pangs of a new Middle East" based on Israeli-Arab cooperation against Iran. Simultaneously, the war transformed al-Qaeda from a small transnational terrorist network into a deeply rooted mass insurgency that could fight and kill Americans on the field of battle. And the revelations about U.S. abuses of Iraqi prisoners at Abu Ghraib prison fueled a surge of anti-American sentiment across virtually the entire region.

However, Iraq was only one part of a much larger transformation of the region. It is difficult to exaggerate the extent to which the post-2001 period increased America's presence in the region. Where only two decades earlier the United States had primarily worked from offshore, it now became intimately involved in security and politics in unprecedented ways. The Global War on Terror globalized the battlefield, leading the U.S. to cooperate closely with Middle Eastern intelligence services in the pursuit, interrogation, and often torture of suspected al-Qaeda militants. The accompanying "war of ideas" led Washington to call for significant changes in the most intimate areas of government and society: religious doctrines, educational curricula, media content, and more. The short-lived "freedom agenda" prescribing democracy as the cure for extremism saw the United States pushing for elections and supporting civil society organizations and oppositional political movement; that it retreated from democracy when opposition forces such as Egypt's Muslim Brotherhood or Palestine's Hamas did well only made Washington look more hypocritical.

Arguments about American "retreat" from the Middle East typically use this exceptional half decade as their baseline for a normal level of U.S. engagement with the region. But it is worth recalling how historically exceptional the moment was, and how short-lived it proved to be. David Petraeus' famous surge of U.S. troops into Iraq from 2006–08 was intended to be temporary, a stopgap measure toward a U.S. drawdown. The costs and failures of Iraq had soured the American public on interventions in the Middle East. The Obama campaign made withdrawal from Iraq a central plank, and once in power moved carefully toward a full withdrawal. The freedom agenda faded away as democracy promotion lost its luster and authoritarian allies regained their purchase. Washington largely gave up on promoting Israeli-Palestinian peace, leaving the situation to drift toward ever faster Israeli settlements and Palestinian political stagnation.

Obama: From the Arab uprisings to the Iran nuclear deal

The Obama administration saw its mission as picking up the pieces from the wreckage of the Bush administration's excess. It scaled back the worst excesses of the War on Terror, began a gradual withdrawal from Iraq, and sought to rebuild American relations with the moderate Muslim majority through a major speech in Cairo. But the administration's regional experience would be most profoundly shaped by the 2011 eruption of the Arab uprisings, which revealed the limitations of not only U.S. primacy in the region but also of its ability to rely on its autocratic allies to maintain order.

Today, after a decade of failures and disaster, it is easy to forget how truly revolutionary the first few months of 2011 really were for the Middle East. The protests that began in a small town in the Tunisian periphery quickly escalated to mass demonstrations across the country, ultimately leading to the longtime President Zine el-Abedine Ben Ali fleeing the country. Coverage of Tunisia's revolution on the Qatari pan-Arab television station Al Jazeera, and excited discussions among young Arabs on social media, turbocharged political excitement everywhere in the Arab world. When Egyptians took to the streets on January 25, and less than three weeks later overthrew President Hosni Mubarak, a fever gripped the entire region. Mass protests hit almost every Arab city, from Morocco to Yemen; only the wealthiest countries (such as Qatar, the UAE, and Saudi Arabia) and the most recently traumatized (Algeria, Iraq) avoided mass mobilization.

The Arab uprisings were primarily driven by domestic concerns, by frustration with nondemocratic and corrupt regimes, and by the pressures of grinding economic woes. But the fully regional nature of the uprising, spreading across more than a dozen countries, deeply challenged what protestors understood to be the American-led regional order. They came at a time when American material power and international prestige had been badly damaged by the toxic legacies of Iraq and the war on terror, as well as by the global financial crisis that had devastated economies across the world. These autocratic and abusive regimes were almost universally American-backed, and it was the U.S. that underwrote the regional order enabling autocracy and corruption to flourish. While the Obama administration initially attempted to align the U.S. with the popular aspirations for freedom and democracy, it ran headlong into the reality that the leaders threatened with overthrow were its own allies.

In that revolutionary moment, regional powers began to take matters into their own hands, intervening widely in pursuit of their own interests and often acting against U.S. preferences. In Egypt, the UAE and Saudi Arabia backed a military coup against the elected Islamist President Mohammed el-Morsi, while in Tunisia they encouraged the rise of an anti-Islamist coalition to combat the Islamist Ennahda Party. The wealthy Gulf states provided financial and political support to less-wealthy fellow monarchs in Oman, Jordan, and Morocco, and directly intervened in support of the embattled Bahraini monarchy, helping to clear the streets by force as the regime launched a campaign of sectarian repression. The Gulf states also took the lead in pushing for military intervention in Libya and Syria. In some of these countries, the Gulf states acted jointly with Washington, namely in Yemen, where the U.S. cooperated closely with Saudi Arabia on a plan for transition away from President Ali Abdullah Saleh. But in many of the key cases—especially Egypt—the UAE and Saudi Arabia in particular worked directly against American policies in ways that threw U.S. leadership into sharp question.

These interventions quickly evolved

Protestors gather in Tahrir Square on February 1, 2011, in Cairo, Egypt. Protests in Egypt continued with the largest gathering yet, with many tens of thousands assembling in central Cairo, demanding the ouster of Egyptian President Hosni Mubarak. PETER MACDIARMID/GETTY IMAGES

THE U.S. AND THE MIDDLE EAST

into fierce competition for influence among these regional powers, with devastating, polarizing effects. The emergence of this intense competition among regional powers, with the United States often seemingly fading into the background, is one of the most important dynamics of the post-2011 period. It is critical to understand why U.S. allies took this path of open defiance. The alliance between the U.S. and Arab allies had long been based primarily on the U.S. guarantee of security, not just from external attack, but also from internal overthrow. Leaders of the Middle East overwhelmingly prioritize regime survival, creating a direct link between their international alliances and their domestic autocratic rule. In 2011, Arab leaders saw their worst nightmares manifest. Washington's rhetorical embrace of democratic change in Egypt and Tunisia frightened and enraged its other autocratic allies, who worried that they too might be abandoned should major protests erupt in their capitals. These doubts about American support for autocrats grew when the U.S. hesitated to intervene directly in Syria to overthrow the regime of Bashar al-Assad, and escalated even more when the Obama administration began direct negotiations with Iran over its nuclear program. All of these policies signaled to regional leaders that Washington was abandoning them, despite all U.S. efforts to reassure them of its ongoing commitment to regional stability and security.

The NATO military intervention in Libya initially represented a high mark of cooperation in the early era of Arab uprisings. Where the Gulf states and the United States disagreed about so much else, they shared a distaste for Libya's eccentric leader Moammar al-Qaddafi. But Libya exposed the limits of their shared vision: America cared about the impending slaughter of opposition forces in Benghazi and hoped to keep the Arab uprisings alive by preventing Qaddafi from killing his way out of the crisis; most Arab rulers wanted to see their eccentric rival toppled, but cared less about him killing his own people and had little interest in seeing the popular revolutions continue. Despite these differences, the combination of Arab support for an intervention against Qaddafi and the reality of impending humanitarian catastrophe proved enough to cement the widest military coalition in the region since the Gulf war. But even here, regional leaders noted the American preference to "lead from behind," offering technical support and air power, but steadfastly refusing to deploy any troops inside of Libya. While Qaddafi was ultimately toppled, and a shaky democracy formed, the shocking assassination of U.S. Ambassador Christopher Stephens a year later and the country's rapid degeneration into civil war and state failure proved a cautionary tale to Washington. In his memoir, Barack Obama singled out the aftermath of the Libya intervention as one of his greatest foreign policy regrets, a sentiment that clearly hung over subsequent decisions in Syria.

As bad as Libya became over the following few years, it was Syria that became the catastrophic epicenter of a broader regional inferno. Syrian protestors initially found little traction in their calls for protest against Assad, but in mid-March, southern Syrians protested against the brutal police abuse of several children who had scrawled anti-regime graffiti. The protests rapidly spread through Syria's cities. Each violent escalation by the regime drove more people into open revolt. Washington tried to walk a fine line, expressing sympathy with the protestors—most notably when Ambassador Robert Ford publicly visited one of the protesting cities, and later when Obama declared that it was time for Assad to step down—while also signaling that it had no intention of intervening. Syria's emerging opposition leadership, as well as protestors on the ground, tended to hear the first message and not the second, hoping that the recent intervention in Libya would be replicated in Syria if the violence truly got out of hand.

Opposition supporters pray in the rain March 4, 2011, in Benghazi, Libya. Thousands of protesters gathered for Friday prayers and listened to a call to arms to join the fight against the government forces of leader Moammar Qaddafi to the west. JOHN MOORE/GETTY IMAGES

By the end of 2011, diplomacy had run its course. Violence escalated dramatically and the United Nations Security Council failed to endorse a resolution authorizing military intervention. Obama, whose view of the Middle East had been profoundly shaped by the disastrous invasion and occupation of Iraq, was determined to avoid a direct military intervention and keenly skeptical of any escalatory moves that might facilitate such a disaster. The administration considered arming the Syrian opposition as a proxy force, as a middle ground between doing nothing and directly intervening. While Washington deliberated, only funding covert small-scale programs providing non-lethal support to the opposition, the Gulf states and Turkey opened the floodgates. These regional powers shipped vast quantities of weaponry and cash to Syrian opposition factions on the ground. While the United States tried valiantly to coordinate these flows of weapons through a unified political structure, it proved unable to control the efforts of its allies. Qatar, Turkey and Saudi Arabia—the three largest state backers of the Syrian insurgency—saw each other as competitors for control over the opposition and a future post-Assad Syria, and prioritized the success of their own proxies and allies over building a unified strategy. At the same time, massive flows of unregulated cash flooded out of the Gulf directly into the hands of Syrian factions on the ground, mostly going from Islamic charities and religious figures into the most overtly Islamist and conservative Syrian groups.

The results were catastrophic. Over the course of 2012, millions of Syrians were displaced from their homes and almost indescribable destruction inflicted by both the regime's forces and by the different insurgency factions. As the rebels advanced toward Damascus, the Lebanese Shia Islamist movement Hezbollah intervened in support of Assad's regime, further regionalizing the conflict; Iran's Islamic Revolutionary Guard Corps (IRGC) and other Shia proxy militias would soon join the fray as the Syrian conflict rapidly internationalized. Within this chaotic warscape, al-Qaeda in Iraq—rebranded as the Islamic State in Iraq and Syria (ISIS)—surged on both sides of the border, as foreign fighters and weapons flowed easily from western Iraq to eastern Syria. In early 2013, ISIS turned its guns against the other rebels, capturing significant swathes of territory and disrupting the anti-Assad war effort. The growing prominence of jihadists in the opposition only increased American reservations about providing advanced weaponry –a fear that the insurgency's other backers did not seem to share.

In the midst of these alarming developments, credible reports surfaced that the Assad regime had used chemical weapons at large scale against an opposition stronghold in the Damascus suburb of East Ghouta. Obama had previously declared the use of chemical weapons a "red line," and in September 2013—after nearly three years of resisting escalation—the White House began mobilizing support for air strikes and other military action against the Assad regime. European and Middle Eastern allies embraced this promise of more muscular intervention, believing that they would finally see the promised regime change delivered. But in the runup to an intervention, British Prime Minister David Cameron lost a Parliamentary vote in support of war. Obama's efforts to persuade a skeptical Congress divided between anti-Obama Republicans and anti-war Democrats were proving difficult. And Obama himself had second thoughts, as he clearly saw the slippery slope ahead of him from air strikes to an Iraq-style war of regime change. A Russian initiative to secure Syria's compliance with an international plan to disarm and remove its chemical weapons presented an off-ramp, which Obama quickly took. Obama could claim that the threat of war had forced Assad to give up his chemical weapons, a victory for coercive diplomacy. But the only message that Middle Eastern regimes received was that the U.S. had failed to follow through on its commitments—a blow to U.S. credibility that turbocharged the extant trend toward defiantly independent policies and open disregard for American preferences.

It is ironic indeed, then, that less than a year later the United States would launch a major military campaign in Syria—only the target would be the Islamic State, not the Assad regime. Three factors forced Obama's hand: First, the dramatic declaration by ISIS leader Abu Bakr al-Baghdadi of a new Caliphate following the shocking conquest of Mosul, Iraq's second largest city. Second, the rapid momentum of ISIS forces toward Baghdad and Iraqi Kurdistan. And, finally, the threatened slaughter of the fleeing Yezidi community. The United States partnered with the Iraqi government—and quietly cooperated with Iran, the primary external force in post-occupation Iraq—to rebuild the Iraqi military and assist it in a slow, difficult military campaign. The intervention coincided with Russia's brutal direct intervention into Syria in defense of Assad. Russian and American aircraft carefully avoided each other as each carried out massive (and ultimately successful) parallel military campaigns.

Finally, in the midst of this regional turmoil, traditional American policy concerns continued to demand atten-

Syrian anti-government protesters gather in Banias on April 29, 2011, during the "Day of Rage" demonstrations called by activists to pressure President Bashar al-Assad as his regime continued a violent crackdwon on dissent. AFP/GETTY IMAGES

THE U.S. AND THE MIDDLE EAST

tion. In 2013, Obama secretly initiated direct negotiations with Iran over its nuclear program, ultimately resulting in high profile public negotiations and an agreement on the 2015 Joint Comprehensive Plan of Action (JCPOA). These negotiations reflected the high priority Obama placed on preventing Iran from acquiring nuclear weapons, as well as his determination to avoid a catastrophic war with Iran, which he believed would profoundly destabilize the region. While Israel and the Gulf states shared Washington's interest in containing the Iranian nuclear program, they sharply disagreed with the diplomatic approach and worked hard to undermine the talks. The Gulf states in particular viewed Iran's regional activities as a far greater threat than a hypothetical nuclear program, chafing at the exclusion of issues such as Iran's support for Assad in Syria, Hezbollah in Lebanon, Shia militias and political parties in Iraq, and the Houthi rebel movement in Yemen. Obama overcame such resistance, in part by assuaging Gulf concerns through major new arms sales and offering reluctant support for the Saudi-led military intervention in Yemen. While Obama could not get the JCPOA ratified by a hostile Senate as an official treaty, it proved highly successful. Iran complied fully with provisions forcing it to surrender its nuclear materials and allow intrusive international inspections and oversight into its nuclear activities.

Trump

Most observers in the region (as in Washington) assumed that Hillary Clinton would continue the Obama administration's general trajectory in the Middle East. The surprise election of Donald Trump, who had campaigned on bellicose rhetoric hostile toward the Iranian nuclear deal and Muslims but had kept his actual policy positions vague, upended those assumptions. Not everything changed, however. Trump continued the war against the Islamic State that Obama had begun, and mostly emulated his predecessor's aversion to direct U.S. military intervention in the region. Despite his vocal hostility toward Iran, he declined to authorize the military strikes that his hawkish allies at home and in the region advocated. He even pushed to remove U.S. troops from Syria.

U.S. President Donald Trump (C) makes his way to board Air Force One in Riyadh as he and the First Lady head to Israel on May 22, 2017. MANDEL NGAN/AFP/GETTY IMAGES

Still, Trump's election had immediate and wide-ranging repercussions for America's Middle East policy. Trump broke with tradition to make Riyadh his first foreign visit. Almost immediately afterward, Saudi Arabia and the UAE launched a bewildering blockade of Qatar in a dramatic escalation of their post-2011 proxy warfare and political competition. This intra-Gulf escalation was a disaster from the perspective of American interests. Not only was Gulf unity essential for an effective strategy toward Iran, but Qatar housed a major American air base threatened by increased chaos in the region.

The blockade of Qatar had ramifications far beyond the Arabian Peninsula. Proxy competitions between the rival Middle Eastern powers intensified, most notably in Libya, where the UAE and Egypt backed a major offensive led by General Khalifa Haftar against rival factions backed by Turkey and Qatar. Trump's support for the Saudi-UAE coalition also escalated the war in Yemen, as well as its draconian economic blockade, causing tremendous humanitarian suffering while achieving little. His willingness to overlook the Saudi murder of journalist Jamal Khashoggi put an exclamation point on the administration's complete disregard for the human rights and democratic ideals that the United States typically claimed to defend.

Perhaps Trump's most destabilizing decision was to pull the United States out of the JCPOA, despite Iran's full compliance with the agreement, and to impose a new wave of draconian sanctions under the label "maximum pressure." This move seriously damaged America's already-weakened credibility, both in the region and globally. Predictably, the new sanctions failed to compel Iran to agree to new terms. Instead, it resumed enrichment activity and sought ways to circumvent sanctions; by the time Trump left office, Iran was far closer to nuclear weapons capability than ever before. Iran's regional activities only continued to expand, with the controversial U.S. assassination of IRGC commander Qassem Suleimani on Iraqi soil barely making a dent.

Trump's other major Middle East initiative was a full-scale push to achieve Arab-Israeli normalization without resolving the Palestinian issue. Trump took a series of pro-Israeli steps, recognizing Israeli sovereignty over the Golan Heights and moving the U.S. embassy to Jerusalem, while ig-

The Israeli and United States flags are projected on the walls of the ramparts of Jerusalem's Old City to mark one year since the transfer of the US Embassy from Tel Aviv to Jerusalem on May 15, 2019. AHMAD GHARABLI/AFP/GETTY IMAGES

noring the Palestinian leadership. The administration soon unveiled a peace plan, labeled "the deal of the century," which completely ignored Palestinian interests and demands to offer perpetual Israeli control of the West Bank and token Palestinian autonomy; it rapidly disappeared without a trace. More enduring were the Abraham Accords, in which the United Arab Emirates and Bahrain (later joined by Morocco and Sudan) normalized relations with Israel and moved toward an open strategic alliance. The Abraham Accords represented an effort to prove that the Palestinian issue no longer mattered in regional politics and that Israel and the Arab states could—and should—openly cooperate against Iran. While the Abraham Accords proved enduring, and the Biden administration would later embrace and desperately seek to expand them, they proved limited in the face of the recurrent crises between Israel and the Palestinians, especially as an extremely right-wing Israeli government moves toward annexation of the occupied territories.

Ultimately, the most significant decision by the Trump administration for the U.S. role in the Middle East may prove to be neither the JCPOA departure or the Abraham Accords. The war in Yemen was spilling over as Houthi rebels and other Iranian-backed groups increasingly launched missiles and other attacks at targets in Saudi Arabia and the UAE. In 2019, a drone attack presumably carried out by Iran targeted the Abqaiq oil refineries in Saudi Arabia, temporarily shutting down Saudi oil production and shipping. The Trump administration, despite its bellicose rhetoric toward Iran, opted to not retaliate. While that decision likely ended a cycle of escalation that could have ended in disaster, it deeply shocked the Gulf states. If Trump—the most pro-Saudi and hawkish President in history—would not respond militarily to a direct Iranian attack on Saudi oil, then when could the United States ever be counted upon? That moment would undoubtedly spur their moves to diversify their international alliances that unfolded over the next few years.

Today's Middle East: Biden and the next administration

The Biden administration did not dramatically change some of Trump's key policies, but it did preside over a rapid regional de-escalation. Within months of Biden's inauguration, Saudi Arabia and the UAE ended their blockade of Qatar, and shortly thereafter mended ties with Turkey. Early tensions with Saudi Arabia caused by Biden's fierce campaign rhetoric about its human rights record and destabilizing activities soon gave way to a full-scale (and somewhat puzzling) U.S. effort to bring the Saudis into the Abraham Accords. The U.S. did not quickly rejoin the JCPOA, with drawn out negotiations ultimately failing to restore the agreement that had been Obama's crowning achievement. Biden showed no more interest in human rights or democracy than had Trump, and made no serious efforts to push Israel toward making peace with the Palestinians.

The Biden administration therefore opted for a somewhat minimalist strategy in its first two years. It worked quietly to de-escalate most of the region's simmering conflicts. The UAE, Saudi Arabia, and Egypt mostly reconciled their differences with Turkey and Qatar, with the blockade on the latter ending days after Biden took office. Libya's civil war stabilized into an uneasy truce with the country divided between two hostile governments, but for the most part avoiding active fighting. Iran, Saudi Arabia and the UAE, and their partners on the ground, mostly honored a ceasefire in Yemen's intractable war and allowed for some limited humanitarian assistance. The United States failed to rejoin the nuclear agreement with Iran that Trump had abandoned, but did work quietly to reduce tensions and slow down Iran's nuclear enrichment efforts. After some early efforts to hold Saudi Arabia accountable for the assassination of Jamal Khashoggi, Washington pivoted toward an attempt to rebuild bridges with Riyadh.

When Russia invaded Ukraine, it shifted the place of the Middle East within Washington's broader global strategy, which now entailed forming a global coalition in defense of Ukraine and the liberal international order. Most of America's Middle East allies—including Saudi Arabia, the UAE, Turkey, and Israel—chose instead to hedge their bets. The preference of longtime

THE U.S. AND THE MIDDLE EAST

American allies to maintain ties with Russia, even under extreme circumstances, was emblematic of how the global environment had changed from the peak of American primacy. Those changes were even more apparent in the Middle East, where China signed new strategic partnership agreements and investment deals with regional states on a seemingly daily basis. The United States remains the most powerful external actor in the Middle East, but it manifestly is no longer in a position to unilaterally order regional politics. Regional powers today see a multipolar world in which they can diversify their alliances, play external powers against each other in search of a better deal, and openly defy American policies without paying a significant price.

The Biden administration's core strategy in the region, perhaps surprisingly, was to build on Trump's Abraham Accords through a complex deal to normalize relations between Saudi Arabia and Israel. It viewed such a deal as a way to counter China's growing role in the region, rebuild America's strategic relationship with its Gulf allies, and enhance Israel's security; critics warned that a deal that ignored the Palestinian issue would only set the stage for more conflict to come. The critics were soon proved right.

Biden's efforts to rebuild an American-led regional order shattered on October 7, 2023, when Hamas launched a shocking incursion into southern Israel, breaking through the security perimeter to rampage through villages and kibbutzim, killing nearly 2,000 people. Israel responded by imposing a complete blockade on Gaza, cutting off water, power, and food, and carrying out an exceptionally fierce bombing campaign across the densely populated Strip. At the time of this writing, Israeli troops are massed outside of Gaza for an expected land offensive, while conflict escalates across the West Bank and with Hezbollah across the border in Lebanon. America found itself increasingly isolated in its support for Israel as the humanitarian catastrophe became clear, while angry public protests erupted across the rest of the Middle East and Arab leaders rebuffed American calls to support Israel or to accept Gazan refugees.

U.S. President Joe Biden (with Secretary of State Blinken) delivers remarks on the attacks in Israel at the White House, October 7, 2023. YURI GRIPAS/NEWSCOM

Choices for the next administration

What does this new global environment mean for the United States and the Middle East? Does the United States still have enduring interests in the region? And can it secure those interests at a level of political and military commitment that it is willing and able to pay?

Traditionally, three primary interests have engaged the United States in the Middle East: the free and predictable flow of oil at reasonable prices; the security of Israel; and the prevention of threats to the United States, such as Soviet inroads during the Cold War or terrorism and Iranian nuclear weapons in more recent years. Those interests remain. The American economy remains highly sensitive to oil prices, even as it has become a leading energy producer itself. For all the tensions in the U.S.-Israeli relationship, there remains a broad bipartisan commitment to close and strong relations. And Washington continues to work to prevent an Iranian nuclear weapon or a new wave of jihadist terrorism. Within that broad constellation of interests, however, there have been some clear changes in U.S. priorities. Three successive Presidents—Obama, Trump, and Biden—have made clear their belief that America faces greater threats to its vital national interests from China, and that the U.S. should reduce its presence in the Middle East in order to focus on Asia. And all three Presidents have shared a deep interest in avoiding another Iraq-style major war in the Middle East.

But the new global and regional environment complicates all of those assumptions. The world now looks less unipolar than it once did, as China's economic role in the region relentlessly expands and Russia offers a military alternative to the American-led order. Power within the Middle East has shifted to the Gulf, Iran, and Turkey rather than the traditional Arab powers. Almost every Arab regime outside the Gulf sits upon a tinderbox of furious citizens tired with economic struggles and political repression at home and the slaughter of Palestinians abroad. The Israeli-Palestinian conflict, far from being a relic of the past, has proven to once again be the most disruptive and difficult issue facing the region today. And the United States has proven unable to extricate itself from the region despite nearly two decades of efforts in that direction.

THE U.S. AND THE MIDDLE EAST

Discussion questions

1. The United States has traditionally pursued several major interests in the Middle East, including the free flow of oil, the security of Israel, and fighting terrorism. Are these still the most important and relevant issues for the American national interest?

2. The Bush administration's decision to invade Iraq continues to hang over discussions of American Middle East policy. In retrospect, did the overthrow of Saddam Hussein advance the interests of the United States and its regional allies? Did it achieve its objectives?

3. The Arab uprisings of 2011 unleashed a massive wave of protests demanding democracy, justice, and freedom. While those are traditionally considered to be American values, the targest of their rage were almost all American allies. Should the United States prioritize its alliance or its values in the Middle East?

4. The Trump administration negotiated the Abraham Accords normalizing relations between Israel and several Arab states on the premise that the Palestinian issue no longer mattered. Does that assumption seem correct in the aftermath of the October 7, 2023, Hamas attack on Israel and the Israeli war on Gaza which followed?

5. Since at least 1991, the United States has been the dominant power in the Middle East. In recent years, that primacy has been challenged by the rise of China and Russia, declining American involvement, and increasing independence of America's regional allies. Are we now living in a multipolar Middle East, or is the United States still the primary power in the region?

Suggested readings

Michael Oren's **Six Days of War** offers a detailed, compelling narrative of the 1967 war and its aftermath, while Martin Indyk's biography of Henry Kissinger, **Master of the Game,** shows how Washington exploited the 1973 war to cement its primacy. Tom Ricks' **Fiasco** delivers a riveting account of the invasion and occupation of Iraq. Steven Simon's **The Grand Delusion** challenges the assumptions that have underlined America's long involvement in the region. Rashid Khalidi's **The One Hundred Year War on Palestine** offers an authoritative Palestinian perspective on the costs of American primacy.

Kim Ghattas's **The Black Wave** offers a sweeping perspective on the regional impact of the 1979 Iranian revolution. Marc Lynch's **The Arab Uprising** and **The New Arab Wars** detail the transformative effects of ther 2011 Arab revolutions. Mona el-Ghobashy's **Bread and Freedom** offers one the best accounts of the dizzying years of revolution and counterrevolution in Egypt. Christopher Phillips's **The Battle for Syria** gives a dispassionate and sharply analytical account of the region's greatest catastrophe; Rania Abouzaid's **No Turning Back** and Wendy Pearlman's **We Crossed a Bridge and it Trembled** offer profoundly human accounts of the war's devastating effects on Syrian civilians.

Don't forget to vote!
Download a copy of the ballot questions from the Resources page at www.fpa.org/great_decisions

To access web links to these readings, as well as links to additional, shorter readings and suggested web sites,
GO TO **www.fpa.org/great_decisions**
and click on the topic under Resources, on the right-hand side of the page.

Global trade and green energy
by Bud Ward

Wind turbines during a heatwave in Palm Springs, California, on July 14, 2023. Excessive heat warnings and watches were posted across California, Nevada and Arizona, where temperatures neared 120F (49C) in some places, the National Weather Service said. KYLE GRILLOT/BLOOMBERG/GETTY IMAGES

Leading climate scientists worldwide for some five decades have issued increasingly dire warnings about potential global dangers as a result of rapid warming of the Earth's atmosphere.

Their findings have echoed across peer-reviewed journals and professional conferences, and now are penetrating the daily consciousness of many citizens and of their policymakers.

Calendar year 2023 may be viewed by future historians as the breaking point in that long cycle. Record-breaking high summer temperatures across much of the planet have paired with another year of hellacious wildfires across much of Europe and North America, and with severe storms and flooding and parching droughts in other regions. Even with stiff competition for the daily broadcast, cable, and newspaper shrinking "news hole," those events have brought home for many the reality of what by now goes simply as "the climate crisis."

Given its obvious global impacts on the planet's atmosphere—and notwithstanding the immediacy of challenges posed by Russia's war on Ukraine and Hamas's war with Israel—the long-term severity of climate change and the resulting urgency of switching from fossil fuels to renewable energy sources now is encountering issues involving international commerce and trade. They relate to each other in vexing ways that some experts fear could impede much-needed short-term climate progress. The nexus between the rush for renewables and the seeming intransigence of international trade issues conspires to create a witch's brew of potential obstacles that could delay, or perhaps even preclude, needed progress in preserving Earth's climate, on which all people, animals, plants, and more rely.

BUD WARD *is an environmental journalist and journalism educator in the Washington, D.C./Virginia area. A co-founder of the Society of Environmental Journalists (SEJ) in 1989, he has authored/co-authored two books on environmental regulatory issues and has authored more than 1,000 bylined articles on environmental and journalism issues. He has served as a regular environmental analyst for National Public Radio's "All Things Considered" and "Morning Edition." In recent years he has conducted a series of full-day workshops for journalists, editors, and broadcast meteorologists on issues related to journalism and climate change science.*

Trade is an essential component of any credible effort to manage the risks of a warming climate, especially in an era defined by conflict between "open trade" and economic protectionism. Adding to the dilemma are a wide range of emerging and established geopolitical tensions that threaten to scuttle meaningful climate change management efforts.

This text first explores some of the factors driving the global effort to move away from fossil fuels. It then digs into some of the key issues involving trade in "rare earth" metals pivotal to building more renewable energy options. After a review of the most important clean energy options, it dives into the geopolitical issues that may be decisive in determining the efforts to decarbonize the global economy.

Renewables

Frequent use of the term "renewable energy" over the past years conjures up images of solar energy and of wind turbines, both onshore and off. That's only logical, but there are other energy sources that show promise: Specifically, nuclear energy and hydroelectric power may play a load-bearing role in future green energy production as well as hydrogen, which received a large investment from the U.S. Department of Energy.

But let solar and wind power—both of which will be subject to the whims of international trade forces—stand in as surrogates for the full range of new and advanced energy resources that are potential successors to fossil-fueled energy.

Solar and wind indeed have some interesting similarities, along with important differences, that distinguish them from each other and from other renewables and, most assuredly, from fossil fuels: They do not release climate-warming pollutants, and, as they replace use of fossil fuels, they can lead to reductions in the rate of increasing atmospheric temperature.

! Before you read, download the companion **Glossary** that includes definitions, a guide to acronyms and abbreviations used in the article, and other material. Go to **www.fpa.org/great_decisions** and select a topic in the Resources section. (Top right)

Importantly, solar and wind enjoy another quality that distinguishes them from fossil fuels: Market prices for both solar and wind energy resources have declined markedly over the past decade, making them economically competitive to fossil fuels in most markets worldwide. It's a trend that the International Energy Agency (IEA) and other climate and energy experts see continuing.

Along with increased use of solar and wind energy comes a need for better battery storage, reserving energy for when and where it is most needed. Improved battery storage, weight reduction, and alternatives are fruitful, and in some cases promising, areas of ongoing research internationally.

Think of it this way: Those old enough to remember may readily recall the classic one-word sentence from the 1967 movie, "The Graduate," starring Dustin Hoffman and Anne Bancroft: "Plastics." Were that movie to be made anew in 2024, the term du jour might well be "Batteries."

Key clean energy options

The IEA outlines where it thinks things are headed:

■ Electricity becomes the core of the energy system.

It will play a key role across all sectors, from transport and buildings to industry. Electricity generation sources will need to reach net zero emissions globally in 2040 and be well on its way to supplying almost half of total energy consumption.

This will require huge increases in electricity system flexibility and network demand response, relying on batteries, nuclear power, hydrogen-based fuels, hydropower, and more—to ensure base and peak load power and reliable supplies.

Let's consider individually these three pillars of renewable energy—solar power, wind power, and battery storage—beginning with an explanation of key factors expected to rise in the context of international trade.

Solar Energy

Ongoing reductions in costs of solar energy make it the leading renewable energy option for decarbonizing the energy economy and for "onshoring" U.S. energy production. Incentives resulting from the Inflation Reduction Act further induce more shifting to solar power, with Princeton University's "Rapid Energy Policy Evaluation and Analysis Toolkit" forecasting increased solar spending to about $321 billion by 2030.

Behind the numbers supporting substantial growth in solar energy are some widely accepted perceptions about solar:

As the most abundant energy source on Earth, the sun's energy is said to be sufficient to power humanity's energy consumption needs for a full year with the solar energy reaching Earth in just 90 minutes.

Energy from the sun is widely accepted as being reliable into perpetuity. From about 0.06% of the planet's energy mix in 2010, solar has grown to about 22% in 2020, providing more than 3% of global electricity generation.

Perhaps more than any other single factor, solar energy costs have shrunk substantially in recent decades, with further declines of more than 30% anticipated in the near future.

Those factors aside, it's generally accepted as a truism in the energy field that "there is no perfect energy source." For solar, the most widely circulated concern is that the sun doesn't always shine, with the implication that no sun means no solar energy. That's where battery storage of solar energy enters the dialogue.

Another concern often expressed is that solar power plants require acres and acres of land, rely on large volumes of water, and use hazardous materials that can present disposal issues. The Covid-19 pandemic illustrated that supply chain problems and rising costs of some components, such as aluminum, can reduce solar expansion. Again, there's no "perfect" energy source.

GLOBAL TRADE AND GREEN ENERGY

Wind energy

That truism applies also to wind energy. With blades that can be 200 feet long, the 100-foot-tall turbines pose aesthetics concerns for some nearby communities and residents, especially when producing annoying whirring background noise. Siting concerns often accompany announced plans for new wind turbines, though once-common worries about their killing hundreds or thousands of birds have mellowed as actual numbers have gone down, largely a credit to changing windmill technologies.

While offshore sitings of wind energy turbines often generate years-long controversies among coastal residents and businesses, they can typically generate more electricity with fewer turbines than onshore turbines.

Again, like solar, costs of wind energy have decreased markedly over recent years relative to costs of fossil fuels, and these cost advantages, as with solar, are expected to continue for years ahead.

Increasing use of renewable energy

U.S. green electricity production is growing. Despite slackened growth in 2022 resulting from higher costs, project delays, supply chain disruption, higher global and domestic inflation rates, and the legacy of a global pandemic, the U.S. added 5.7 gigawatts (GW) of utility-scale solar generation capacity and 7 GW of wind capacity compared with the same eight-month period through August a year earlier. The two resources' combined share of U.S. electricity generation increased to 23% from 21% during the same period of 2021, according to the U.S.'s national renewable energy industry outlook.

Energy experts overwhelmingly point to solar and wind as the renewables most likely to increase in market share relative to other renewables and fossil fuels over the next decade. While nuclear energy is also expected to grow, many experts think nuclear energy is unlikely to increase its current (roughly 10%) global market share over the next several decades. The reasons? Unfavorable cost comparisons to renewables, difficulties in nuclear waste handling and disposal, long construction lead times, and, in some countries, widespread anxieties about security and safety.

"By 2050, the energy world looks completely different," the International Energy Agency (IEA) reports. "Global energy demand is around 8% smaller than today, but it serves an economy more than twice as big and a population with 2 billion more people. Almost 90% of electricity generation comes from renewable sources, with wind and solar PV [photovoltaics] together accounting for almost 70%. Most of the remainder comes from nuclear power."

Looking ahead about three decades, the IEA says, "Solar is the world's single largest source of total energy supply. Fossil fuels fall from almost four fifths of total energy supply today to slightly over one fifth. Fossil fuels that remain are used in goods where the carbon is embodied in the product such as plastics, in facilities fitted with carbon capture, and in sectors where low-emissions technology options are scarce."

Brookings Institution researchers Kemal Davis and Sebastian Strauss, in a February 2021 commentary, write that reaching net zero* by 2050 "is technically and economically feasible with existing and in-progress technologies." But they added an important qualifier: "It requires drastic shifts in behavior and massive policy interventions, including a degree of international cooperation that will be very difficult to attain."

Nuclear Energy

No serious discussion of alternative or additional energy sources is complete without consideration of domestic nuclear power.

That has, in fact, long been the case, notwithstanding strong public attitudes generally opposing nuclear plants—or the disposal of nuclear wastes—near residential communities ("Not in my back yard!").

Proponents of expanded nuclear energy make the persuasive case that nuclear energy is cleaner than combustion of coal or oil. They maintain that nuclear power, especially advanced nuclear power options, must not be summarily dismissed, given widespread and serious concerns over global warming and the inability of solar and wind to provide base power for the electrical grid.

Some proponents of nuclear energy acknowledge that the production stage required to scale nuclear energy may raise some legitimate concerns over environmental problems. Again, there's no "perfect" energy source.

However, many experts do not put substantial weight in arguments that the use of nuclear power for energy generation need necessarily lead to increased risks of nuclear weapons proliferation, another concern of some opposing nuclear powered-adversaries. But even if such worries were somehow taken off the table, major concerns persist about the exceptionally high costs associated with nuclear power, particularly relative to renewables, and about siting and permitting delays contributing to unavoidably lengthy and drawn-out lead times for construction.

It's not uncommon to hear mentions that popular support for nuclear energy could increase significantly *only* if the feared most adverse consequences of global warming themselves become widely unacceptable to the public and elected representatives and civic leaders.

Few responsible speculators at this point can argue unequivocally that that last turn of events is itself inconceivable. In that case, support for nuclear energy indeed could increase.

Only time will tell.

---

*The term 'net zero' in the context of climate change means reaching a balance between carbon emitted into the atmosphere and carbon removed from it. 'Net zero' is achieved when no more carbon is released than is removed from the atmosphere.

David Yeager, project manager for Vistra Zero, looks over the battery array in the old generator building at the Moss Landing Power Plant in Moss Landing, Calif., on January 13, 2021. Vistra Zero is the largest energy storage system of its kind in the world, able to store up to 300Mw of power. It uses lithium-ion batteries to capture excess electricity from the grid and release it when needed later, typically during solar and wind down times. CARLOS AVILA GONZALEZ/THE SAN FRANCISCO CHRONICLE/GETTY IMAGES

Increased battery storage

Solar and wind do bear a common characteristic: The sun doesn't always shine, and the winds don't always blow. Both renewable energy sources depend on batteries to store energy. With adequate storage, the cloudy days impediment and the absence of winds need not be prohibitive concerns. Batteries remain a key linchpin in the evolution to clean energy sources.

Battery storage is critical not only as it applies to the needs of stationary facilities, but also to support transportation activities.

"The next decade will be big for energy storage in general and for batteries in particular," says Prescott Hartshorne, a director of National Grid Ventures, which does energy and energy storage work in the U.S. and the U.K. "Storage enables further renewable generation both from an operational and reliability perspective. It's also a key piece of our utility customers' ongoing evolution and transition to renewables."

Research efforts across the planet are aimed at both increasing battery storage capacity and, especially in the production of electric vehicles (EVs), suppressing both the weight and the cost of batteries.

"Battery storage capacity in the United Sates was negligible prior to 2020, when electricity storage capacity began growing rapidly," the U.S. Energy Information Administration (EIA), says in a December 2022 report. "The remarkable growth in U.S. battery storage capacity is outpacing even the early growth of the country's utility-scale solar capacity," the agency continues. "U.S. solar capacity began expanding in 2010 and grew from less than 1.0 GW in 2010 to 13.7 GW in 2015…Much like solar power, growth in battery storage would change the U.S. electric generating portfolio."

Increased battery storage capacity can help solve an "intermittency problem," storing extra energy produced by wind or solar generators for when that energy is most needed. The EIA reports that developers are planning more than 23 large-scale battery projects—ranging from 250 megawatts to 650 megawatts—by 2025.

Lithium-ion batteries are the leading storage technology for those large plants, but the whole range of battery storage technologies is expected to remain an area of active research for years to come. It's reasonable to expect significant technological changes involving batteries and storage in coming years.

Conundrum of rare earth metals/minerals

The following points, drawn largely from the World Bank report, illustrate some of the issues to be addressed in bringing about the hoped-for smooth transition to carbon-free energy options. Remember here that the specific rare metals now thought essential in this transition must be application-specific: what works for "green" wind energy may be totally unsuitable for solar or for battery storage, and vice versa. Furthermore, what makes sound economic sense in a global warming goal of no more than a two-degree Celsius warming increase may be off-the-charts expensive in limiting warming to 1.5 degrees Celsius.

Key metals

Solar Technologies—Four widely used technologies prevail for building solar photovoltaic (PV) cells:
- crystalline silicon cells, comprising roughly 85% of the current market;
- copper aluminum selenide (CIGS), a "thin film" technology with potential material reduction and manufacturing advantages;
- cadmium telluride, also a thin film technology, with some competitive cost advantages, but with highly toxic cadmium and questionable future supplies of tellurium; and
- amorphous silicon of amorphous silicon-germanium cells, the remaining "thin film" technology, but suffering from lower performance.

The 2015 market share of all thin film technologies was about 8% of the total annual production. The four solar technologies' significant metal content differs widely.

"The balance between these [solar energy] technologies has huge implications for metals such as indium, silver,

GLOBAL TRADE AND GREEN ENERGY

and zinc," the World Bank report notes. Estimating future demand for those technologies "will define the demand for a wide range of metals."

Energy storage batteries—This application includes lead-acid, lithium-ion, and "other" categories including various battery chemistries: nickel-metal-hydride and sodium-sulfur and non-battery storage such as pumped-storage hydro, flywheels, and hydrogen.

The more established technology involves lead-acid batteries, historically less costly than lithium-ion batteries but having poor power-to-weight and energy-to-weight ratios.

Lithium-ion batteries have excellent energy-to-weight ratios, and prices have been decreasing significantly.

Wind Power—Larger turbine sizes and economies of scale in recent years have reduced generation prices, making wind, like solar, competitive with fossil fuels generation. Electricity production generated by wind power, especially for on-shore rather than off-shore wind, is expected to increase "rapidly" over the next three decades. (The World Bank cites evidence of "overly conservative estimates of expected penetration levels of renewable technologies."

Two wind technologies exist for the wind industry market, with differing needs for metals. Offshore wind turbines, expected to rely "almost completely" on direct-drive design, are estimated to be about 50% of total installed generation capacity by 2050. "But the split between onshore and offshore installations, and even between geared and direct-drive installations in these two locations, remains uncertain."

An illustrative problem

Despite the clear need for more renewable energy sources, a series of technical, economic, and political obstacles block the way.

One of the most illustrative concerns in the production of green energy infrastructure is the need for vastly increased mining of rare earth metals. These metals are essential to the production of electric vehicles and more advanced batteries, both of which are necessary innovations in a reduced-carbon infrastructure. The challenge facing the U.S. in a nutshell: Several of the key metals—nickel and cobalt, and bauxite as a key component of aluminum—are found in countries and regions adversarial to U.S. interests. Even in countries amenable to U.S. interests, the mining and extraction of these metals pose serious environmental, water quality, and public health risks for local workers and populations.

With the increasing demand for rare earth metals and ores (such as nickel, lithium, and cobalt), policy makers and the public will need to be sensitive to a range of critical questions, the answers to which in many cases will depend on factors such as:

■ Which rare earth metals are best suited for which specific applications?
■ Which individual countries have the largest and most accessible supplies of the individual metals?
■ How and whether those individual countries will be open or resistant to making those resources available to other countries, and at what cost?
■ For which such prized resources are there now, or might there soon be, suitable substitutes or other options available at commercial scale, and, again, at what cost?

Looking ahead, rare earth metals will be a critical component in more efficient and cleaner renewable energy and increased battery storage options. Notwithstanding their essential utility to the energy transition, these metals also present some specific challenges in how they are accessed and used.

"Known unknowns" and "unknown unknowns," to borrow from former U.S. Secretary of Defense Donald Rumsfeld, loom large in discussions addressing the building blocks to the global transition to carbon-free energy.

Given the innumerable uncertainties in any "smooth" transition, it's notable that, as a World Bank report says, "little attention has been paid to the implications of growing demand for materials required in the construction of renewable technologies and zero-emission infrastructure." The report draws a contrast to the volumes written about declining demand for fossil fuels, in particular coal, in such a transition.

Especially notable when considering the shift from a fossil-fuels-driven economy toward a "green energy" future is the consensus noted by the World Bank that:

"All literature examining material and metals implications for supplying

Street vendors at Conkary's Petit Bateau commuter train station walk next to wagons used to transport bauxite from the mining areas to Guinea's main port in Conakry's Kaloum neighbourhood. Despite a wealth of valuable minerals like diamonds, gold, and aluminum ore, Guinea ranks as one of the poorest countries in the world. Only about a third of residents have access to electricity, and the country's 32% literacy rate is among the lowest in the world. JASON FLORIO/REDUX

Other strategies: carbon capture and sequestration, and geoengineering

Carbon capture and sequestration (CCS) and, separately, geoengineering, are two critical climate management strategies that must be considered both in the context of climate change and of related international trade matters.

There are two types of CCS. The first involves the extraction of greenhouse gases directly from the air, after which they are deposited underground or otherwise stored. The second involves the capture of emissions from the combustion of fossil fuels, such as from power plants or industrial facilities.

The ideal "net-zero" goal of climate change management is to eliminate the use and, thereby, the atmospheric emissions of fossil fuels. No combustion (in effect, stranding trillions of dollars' worth of fossil fuels in the earth) would mean no emissions. However, progress in that direction notwithstanding, what then of the emissions from those fuels that are burned while in the transition to renewables?

In those cases, CCS, and perhaps also at some point geoengineering, may make up the difference. Note that CCS itself consists of two key components—first capture, and then sequestering where the carbon cannot be released into the atmosphere. Both of those components pose as-yet-unresolved challenges.

CCS involves capturing carbon dioxide (CO_2) after combustion so it can be stored permanently and not released into the atmosphere. Underground geological formations are critical here. CCS of this sort is nothing new: it's been used at various locations and in varying amounts worldwide. Some commercial-scale facilities already operate throughout the world, with more in planning stages. Far more still will be needed.

Of course, CCS has its proponents and its opponents. While some see CCS as a way to help justify continued production of oil, others argue that it incentivizes the continuation of combustion that might otherwise give way to renewable energy sources.

There are technical, technological, permitting and siting, and economic barriers impeding further applications of CCS. Furthermore, some harbor concerns that no "permanent" underground storage may really be permanent, perhaps leading to future leaks.

There are different "flavors" of CCS also to consider, some inevitably having higher demands for technological components or specific building blocks than others. Biological carbon sequestration can take place in soils and oceans. With oceans, cooler and nutrient-rich waters can absorb more carbon dioxide than warmer seas, a potential concern given that oceans generally are getting warmer and more acidic specifically because of climate change.

Through photosynthesis, University of California Davis researchers have pointed out, carbon can be sequestered and stored as soil organic carbon, opening the way for storage of carbon through "new land management with calcium and magnesium minerals, forming 'caliche' in desert and arid soil." Efforts are under way to accelerate the carbonate forming process, using finely crushed silicates in the soil to store carbon for longer time periods.

Forests and grasslands also can serve as valuable "carbon sinks." Fallen leaves and branches store carbon, but they also can pose fire concerns, reducing forests' potential for carbon sequestration. Grasslands, somewhat more resilient, have the advantage of storing most carbon underground.

Carbon stored in underground geological formations can be derived from industrial sources producing steel or cement, or from power plants or natural gas facilities. The carbon in these cases is injected into porous rocks for storage.

Extensive ongoing research into CCS is continuing throughout the world as concerns about increasing climate change risks intensify.

Geoengineering

Geoengineering the climate generally amounts to deliberate and long-term modification of the planet and its natural systems to reduce global warming. In the context of climate change, the term does not include short-term regional efforts such as cloud-seeding, undertaken to increase rainfall in a region over the short term.

As with CCS, there are variations of geoengineering: Broadly, they focus on methods of solar radiation management, SRM, which involves reducing the amount of solar radiation, sunlight, reaching earth's surface. This reduction is brought about by the injection of various chemicals into the upper atmosphere.

Not so many years ago, it almost seemed that the subject of geoengineering the atmosphere was verboten in pleasant company, especially when discussants included scientists.

Generally dismissed as a "break-glass" worst case scenario, not even close to being a "Plan B," the mere researching of geoengineering options was readily dismissed as being too fraught with unwanted and unintended consequences: Adamant critics warned that the research alone could open doors to actual implementation, thereby fueling more pollution of the sort the geoengineering was intended to help reverse.

Only if the adverse impacts of climate change become so unequivocally serious and damaging, this logic flows, might one resort to such a serious remedy. Its consequences? Unknown and in many ways unknowable, but certainly negative. Regional and local climate impacts such as flooding, droughts, or wildfires seem inevitable. And it's generally accepted that geoengineering, once launched at a global scale, must be continued indefinitely, and surely for more than 100 years. As such, geoengineering raises some serious ethical, equity, and moral concerns not easily resolved. It would be, at best, a dubious gift to our heirs and to future generations.

(For more information on these climate strategies, see Topic 3)

clean technologies agrees strongly that building these technologies will result in considerably more material-intensive demand than would traditional fossil fuel mechanisms."

Knowing the specific rare elements/metals likely to experience increasing market shares in a carbon-free economy is just the first part of the challenge. The real uncertainties arise concerning the carbon-free technologies for which they will be deployed, the timing involved in the transitions to each, and, in some important cases, the specific applications within each category and the known locations of ample deposits, vast amounts of which are located in China. *The Economist* reports that "The transition to clean energy will spark decades of demand for the metals needed to multiply solar and wind parks, power lines, and electric cars. Latin America holds more than a fifth of the global reserves for five critical metals" and "already dominates the mining of copper, pervasive across green technologies, and holds nearly 60% of the world's known resources of lithium, used in all main e-vehicle battery types." Also, there's the issue of the geographic sites at which suitable, accessible, and economical supplies will be available.

In addition to issues of which rare metals fit with which green technologies and in what time frame, there also are concerns related to which countries' rare metal resources are accessible in the first place—and at what economic and environmental costs. This is where trade and economic factors and potential political and environmental, health, and safety regulatory concerns will come up, in some cases facilitating trade with particular countries while impeding it with others.

For instance, bauxite ore is a principal component of aluminum, a metal subject to increasing demand as part of efforts to trim unnecessary weight from electric vehicles, EVs, and their batteries. *The Washington Post* reports that Guinea, "one of the poorest countries on earth," sits on "the world's biggest reserve of bauxite." Home to more than 13 million people, Guinea also is "already seeing an unprecedented boom in its bauxite exports" given growing global interest in EVs. At what expense? Guinea already reports a loss of farmland, reduced crop yields, and devastated fishery harvests resulting from mining activities and development. Furthermore, locals face serious drinking water quality problems following the bauxite mining initiatives.

Other countries in the Global South may face, or already face, similar problems. "The Latin America region (Chile, Brazil, Peru, Argentina, and potentially Bolivia) is in an excellent position to supply the global climate-friendly energy transition," according to the World Bank. "The region has a key strategic advantage in copper, iron ore silver, lithium, aluminum, nickel, manganese, and zinc," and along with Africa "should also serve as a burgeoning market for these resources."

Again, examples from among many already apparent:

An April 27, 2023, report in *The Washington Post* illustrates the dilemma, beginning "One of the poorest countries on Earth has become a crucial player in the world's green-energy transition." It continues:

"Guinea, a West African nation of more than 13 million people, is home to the world's biggest reserves of bauxite—a reddish-brown rock that is the main source of aluminum. That light metal, in turn, is essential for electric vehicles because it allows them to travel farther without recharging than if they were made of steel. And over the current decade, when experts expect global sales of EVs to increase almost ninefold, demand for aluminum will jump nearly 40%, to 119 million tons annually, industry analysts say."

The article reports that Guinea's government "has reported that hundreds of square miles once used for farming have been acquired by mining companies for their operations and associated roads, railways, and ports." Villagers "have received little or no compensation." In the next two decades, the paper reports based on government analyses, "more than 200,000 acres of farmland and 1.1 million acres of natural habitat will be destroyed by bauxite mining."

More than half of the world's lithium, critical for battery storage for electric vehicles, comes from Latin America, as does roughly 40% of the world's copper and some 25% of its nickel. A form of "green-resource nationalism," as *The Economist* describes it, is taking place in some countries in the region, along with rising interest in export bans of nickel ore and of bauxite, the latter critical in making aluminum and for reducing weights—and thereby increasing mileage—of electric vehicles and of energy-storage batteries.

The proverbial game-changer on this issue, however, is China, given the global dominance the country enjoys on metals (both basic and rare earth), solar panels, and services required to supply technologies in a carbon-constrained future. The World Bank, in its report, writes that China's "production and reserve levels, even when compared with resource-rich countries (such as Canada and the United States, and to a lesser extent Australia) often dwarf others."

Bottom line: A lot depends on which technologies gain prominence, and where and when, over the next few decades. Much also relies on how readily, if at all, key countries make their rare earth resources available beyond their own borders. There are constant efforts in renewable system research and design to reduce the need for rare earth metals and minerals that are difficult and/or expensive to access and then to procure.

Will consumers and vehicle-makers worldwide tilt demand toward all-electric vehicles, thereby increasing need for more bauxite, cobalt, copper and lithium? Or will existing inventories of aging "gas guzzlers" hold out against new EVs? For how long? Will various national governments succeed in incentivizing selection of EVs? And, if not, what roles might the private sector adopt to help fill voids? And, finally, as seen from the United Auto Workers' 2023 strike against the traditional "big three" automakers, what might be the economic and political impacts of EVs' requiring fewer manufacturing and service workers across the board than required by fossil-fuel powered vehicles?

Geopolitical issues involving clean-energy transition

For many, questions about climate change have evolved over the years from a focus on whether and if… to a focus on what to do about the serious climate challenges we now face: What kinds of policies might best incentivize practical and effective risk management actions?

As the IEA says in its annual World Energy Outlook for 2022, "the risks of further energy disruption and geopolitical fragmentation are high." Those risks must now be addressed in the context of a ticking clock that experts say calls for effective actions sooner rather than later.

As the long-debated underlying scientific evidence for years had been, the public policy options can be complex and controversial. Many can elicit the "now comes the hard part" reaction in addressing the what-when-and-how of policy action choices confronting modern societies worldwide.

In addition, geopolitical issues certainly will evolve and change over time, complicating any coordinated international efforts set in motion today. Sometimes, those changes can develop rapidly, as, for instance, with Russia's invasion of Ukraine and its impacts on global energy and food supplies, and President Biden's recent executive order restricting semiconductor trade with China.

In contrast, rapid changes are un-

How two of the U.S.'s most highly respected climate scientists view clean energy geopolitics

Richard B. Alley, Ph.D., of Penn State University, and Lonnie Thompson, Ph.D., of The Ohio State University, both members of the National Academy of Science, are two of the most honored and respected climate scientists in the U.S. and, indeed, in the world. They offered these remarks when asked by the author of their views on the nexus between climate science and climate policy development.

Dr. Richard B. Alley:

"Solving" climate change has indeed been difficult, but scientific uncertainties have not been truly so important for decades. As documented in many excellent sources, the foundations for understanding global warming from fossil-fuel burning were sketched out during the 1800s. The predictive quantum-mechanical framework of radiative transfer came about from the US Air Force helping target heat-seeking missiles and calculate climate change after World War II. By the time I started helping the United Nations Intergovernmental Panel on Climate Change, IPCC, (in its 1995 report), the main outline of the scientific understanding was taught in widespread undergraduate classes. Scientists were increasingly documenting that the uncertainties are mostly on the "bad" side—if we continue to drive warming, the resulting damages could be a little less or a little more than expected, or a lot more if we trigger abrupt climate changes or ice-sheet collapses or other tipping points.

But despite the rapid rise in use of renewable energy, we continue to rely deeply on fossil fuels. Over recent years in the USA, for example, external use of energy to take care of our heating and cooling, lighting and plowing, and trucking and so much more, has been roughly 100 times as much as what we can do for ourselves from the energy in our food. The great majority of that external energy has come from a fossil-fuel system that has taken more than a century to build in its present form, and that is woven into our communities, our economy, and our politics, with vast resources. "Scientific uncertainty" long has been one of many arguments used and misused in discussions of ways forward to build a truly sustainable energy system, but the science has continued to be accurate and reliable with no major changes in understanding. The scholarship is clear that we can use this accurate science to build a better energy system, helping the economy and the environment if we can get the policies right.

Dr. Lonnie Thompson

Over the last four decades, data from ice cores, glaciers, and other sources have proven that Earth's climate is changing rapidly, and that carbon-based energy use is largely responsible. One of the greatest challenges of the 21st century is dealing with this unprecedented, global-scale change, since virtually all human activities are affected by climatic fluctuations.

We have the potential to transition to carbon-free societies through developing technology to slow carbon-based greenhouse gas emissions, advancing battery technology, and reducing the cost of renewable energy below fossil fuel energy. However, many of these technologies depend on rare earth elements that are most abundant in countries such as China and Russia, both of which at times have adversarial relationships with the U.S. and other countries and also with each other.

Earth's inhabitants now face a slow but inexorably developing crisis in which all nations must cooperate for the ultimate welfare of current and future generations. Despite political and economic rivalries, ultimately the global community must work together to slow the pace of human-caused climate change and to mitigate its worst impacts. Human actions have created the unfolding climatic and environmental crises, but we must implement international policies to make our energy production and consumption sustainable.

heard of concerning basic scientific evidence—for example, that increased emissions of human-caused carbon dioxide emissions further warm the atmosphere, and that elevated concentrations of greenhouse gases in the atmosphere need to be reduced.

Another example of the kind of change that could lead to a different set of geopolitical factors: Scientists are actively seeking effective alternatives to some of the essential metals and ores seen today as irreplaceable. For example, promising research suggests that sodium may someday replace or complement lithium as a key component of energy storage batteries.

Adding further to the challenge is the reality that effective policy responses can involve differing approaches at the local, regional, national, and/or international levels. In some cases, a step taken even by a local or regional government can delay or impede national or international efforts, even if only by leading to drawn-out litigation. "Many a slip twixt the cup and the lip," the familiar English proverb reminds us.

More must be considered also given that actions taken to manage global climate could inflict further damages to the natural environment regionally or locally, potentially increasing public health risks. The concern here is that we appear in some cases to have to further foul local and regional natural resources, such as clean air and finite drinking water supplies and drinking water quality, in order to control the even more perverse adverse impacts of a warmer atmosphere globally.

In such situations, the most serious impacts, as often is the case, are likely to disproportionately affect minority and traditionally underserved populations, the most vulnerable populations. The sad irony is that those groups are precisely those who have played the smallest roles in creating the anthropogenic (human-caused) warming in the first place.

The rift between wealthy and poor countries inevitably will widen.

The 'illusion' of a smooth glide path on energy transition

Geopolitical issues—as they apply specifically to climate change initiatives and to other global efforts—are anything but simple. They often present a numbing mix of uncertainties and unknowns.

Columbia and Harvard University academics Jason Bordoff and Meghan L. O'Sullivan write in *Foreign Affairs* about some "waxing lyrical about the geopolitical benefits of the coming transition to a cleaner, greener energy" and "an end to the troublesome geopolitics of the old energy order."

"Such hopes," they wrote, "were based on an illusion."

They wrote just months after the start of Russia's war with Ukraine that "even the most optimistic evangelist of the new energy order had realized that the transition would be rocky at best."

Why? Because "the energy transition and geopolitics are entangled."

It may yet be tempting for some to boil down the green energy international transition to a very few words: China and the United States. This approach holds that the ultimate successes and/or failures of managing climate change risks will be shaped by the timeliness and effectiveness of actions taken—or not taken—by those two superpowers.

"The return of great-power rivalry in an increasingly multipolar and fragmented international system, the effort of many countries to diversify their supply chains, and the realities of climate change," Bordoff and O'Sullivan wrote in that *Foreign Affairs* piece, will add further stress to meeting the challenges posed by a changing climate. And the nature of the geopolitical issues directly involving just the U.S. and China likely will shape the geopolitics of virtually the entire world. Developments underscoring continued and heightened tensions between the U.S. and China throughout 2023—including and going beyond the future independence of Taiwan—do nothing to lower such concerns.

Will the two leading superpowers, and other powerful countries following suit, approach current and future climate initiatives with an increased commitment to trade protectionism and to nationalism? Will the key countries' international commerce and trade postures be driven by increasing selective taxes or tax credits, tariffs, trade restrictions, barriers, or embargoes? Or might a growing spirit of international accord develop to confront the "common enemy" of an excessively warming atmosphere? Will a growing U.S. and China spirit of cooperation and togetherness incentivize other powerful economic interests—India, Australia, advanced Western European and Pacific countries, Canada, and more—to join such a concerted collaborative effort?

The questions, of course, come

Staff members work at a workshop of a photovoltaic technology company in Yancheng, east China's Jiangsu Province, Sept. 6, 2023. Yancheng has boosted green and low-carbon development by advancing new energy industries such as wind and photovoltaic power in recent years. LI BO/XINHUA/GETTY IMAGES

Tata Steel steel mill close to the North Sea coast on October 5, 2023, in Velsen, Netherlands. Tata steel is one of the major polluters in the Netherlands in terms of CO2, nitrogen, and heavy metals such as lead and mercury. Residents around Tata Steel, formerly Hoogovens, have been concerned for some time about carcinogenic substances falling into the area. SJOERD VAN DER WAL/GETTY IMAGES

more easily than do the well-reasoned answers. Consider, for instance, a few examples of the countless kinds of geopolitical issues and impediments to be addressed and, one can hope, overcome:

■ Saudi Arabia's flirtation with China and Russia and concerns that it may well lead to its being less sympathetic to U.S. interests, given what it and others see as an up and down wavering of the U.S.'s strategic commitment to the Middle East;

■ The increased interest on the part of many countries to enhance and diversify their own energy supply chains—and also simply to foster their own energy supply market shares—in light of their growing concerns about over-reliance on unpredictable foreign sources;

■ Growing concerns among countries over energy security challenges they fear in coming years and decades, both as they may involve the health, productivity, and well-being of their own populations, and as those challenges would affect essential infrastructure resources such as highways, rail transit, public utilities, and health care and agricultural production resources;

■ In the U.S. and other key countries, uncertainties over whether a change in near-term presidential or congressional leadership will lead to substantially different approaches to implementation of, or financial support for, landmark climate provisions of initiatives such as, in the U.S., the climate change provisions of the Inflation Reduction Act.

Even with the inevitable reduction in worldwide use of fossil fuels, Bordoff and O'Sullivan point out, "geopolitical risks may increase as global production becomes further concentrated in countries that can produce at low cost and with low emissions, many of which are in the Persian Gulf." They write that the share of global oil supply by OPEC producers will rise "from around one-third today to roughly one-half" by 2050. They note also an estimate by oil giant BP that the OPEC countries by then will produce a "very high and consequential…large share of a tiny pie," about two thirds of global oil supply "even if annual demand is falling."

One possible approach for the U.S.? "Friend shor-ing": turning to "less risky" friendly countries such as Norway and Canada, and "penalizing less friendly oil sources"—think here Iran, Libya, and Venezuela—with import taxes "or even sanctions." Bordoff and O'Sullivan acknowledge such actions could lead to "backlash and retaliation," such as higher prices and output reductions (for instance of Saudi Arabian oil).

And what about the unintended consequence of a "clean-energy" transition that involves increased adverse environmental and health impacts at local and regional scales, such as releases of polluted water or mining wastes into potable water supplies, or increased emissions of harmful air pollutants? Mining and extraction actions aimed at securing needed amounts of some "rare earth" ores and metals vital to a clean-energy transition have been widely reported as raising serious public health concerns, further evidencing the "no perfect energy source" reality.

In the end, once the scientifically challenging issues are resolved, and once a critical mass of the broad global public commits to seriously addressing climate change, the obstacles potentially presented by geopolitical realities still may long delay or impede effective progress on reducing global climate pollution and avoiding the most serious adverse impacts of a rapidly changing climate. The challenges are clear; the most effective responses to them are less so.

GLOBAL TRADE AND GREEN ENERGY

Discussion questions

1. The transition from a fossil-fuel based economy to an economy overwhelmingly—and perhaps ultimately entirely—based on renewable energy sources is likely to have a devastating economic and societal impact on certain population groups long tied to their familial pasts. What role should national and state governments play in helping to smooth that transition for those—such as coal miners refinery workers and their families—adversely affected by the transition?

2. Nuclear power is seen as a carbon-free energy source versus fossil fuel resources, although critics fairly point to adverse climate impacts resulting from development and transport of nuclear energy resources, though not during combustion. What do you see as the optimum role for domestic nuclear power in a transition to a "net-zero" economy? How can nuclear power overcome some of the most common concerns of critics—high costs, long permitting and construction delays, concerns over national security, and disposal of nuclear wastes?

3. *The Economist* recently framed things this way: "Growth is the best way to lift people out of poverty and improve average living standards. But in the developing world, more growth still leads to more emissions…. It is a battle over what is worse: a poorer today or a hotter tomorrow?" How to weigh the adverse health and environmental impacts on regional population groups today against less obvious adverse impacts for the planet generally in coming years? Are you optimistic or pessimistic about the ability to maintain growth while converting to a net-zero carbon emissions economy? What is your view of *The Economist's* framing of this issue?

5. At a time when protectionism and nationalism appear to be on the increase across a number of countries around the world, how do you see free-trade and "America First" nationalism interests evolving during the early energy transition years? Do you see a period of "natural resources nationalism" impeding global access to rare earth minerals and metals needed to fuel a move to clean electrification?

6. How should the federal government deal with adversarial countries (such as China and Russia) in addressing the "common enemy" of human-caused climate change? Are there effective means of incentivizing cooperative resources trading among erstwhile adversaries? How might the U.S. best deal with friendly/neutral countries such as India and Brazil? Should the U.S. seek to continue taking the international lead in addressing climate change? And, if so, how can it do that?

Suggested readings

The World Bank, April 2023, "Falling Long-Term Growth Prospects: Trends, Expectations, and Policies." The World Bank in this report offers what it says is "the first comprehensive assessment of long-term potential output growth rates in the aftermath of the Covid-19 pandemic and the Russian invasion of Ukraine." The report characterizes these rates as the global economy's "speed limit," which would have significant implications for international commerce on renewable energy and other subjects. https://www.worldbank.org/en/news/press-release/2023/03/27/global-economy-s-speed-limit-set-to-fall-to-three-decade-low?intcid=ecr_hp_sidekick3_en_exT

Intergovernmental Panel on Climate Change (IPCC)—The Intergovernmental Panel on Climate Change, IPCC, is a project of the United Nation Environment Program and the World Meteorological Organization. For decades IPCC has been widely acknowledged as the world's most authoritative voice on climate change science. Its studies are the work of a who's who of the world's leading climatologists, and their work products reflect a comprehensive aggregation of recent years' peer-reviewed journal reports and research.www.ipcc.ch

The Economist, June 25–July 1, 2022. "The Right Way to Fix the Energy Crisis," Some of the most insightful and analytical reporting on climate change regularly appears in the print and online formats of this magazine, and this feature lives up to that viewpoint. Cover story, The Economist, June 25-July 1, 2022. www.economist.com

Resources for the Future, RFF—Global Energy Outlook, May 20, 2023. Climate change watchers each year eagerly await this annual update from a respected national think tank. RFF's report for 2023 aggregates key relevant data from several highly respected national and international sources. The result is sector-by-sector and energy source-by-energy data (wind, solar, nuclear, etc.) and projections into coming decades. www.Rff.org/geo

---

Don't forget to vote!
Download a copy of the ballot questions from the Resources page at www.fpa.org/great_decisions

---

To access web links to these readings, as well as links to additional, shorter readings and suggested web sites,
GO TO **www.fpa.org/great_decisions**
and click on the topic under Resources, on the right-hand side of the page.

Risky science across borders
by Mila Rosenthal

A giant volcanic mushroom cloud explodes from Mount Pinatubo some 12 miles above the almost deserted U.S. Clark Air Base, on June 12, 1991, followed by another more powerful explosion a few days later. The eruption of Mount Pinatubo on June 15, 1991, was the second largest volcanic eruption of the 20th century. ARLAN NAEG/AFP/GETTY IMAGES

Just over 30 years ago, on June 15, 1991, Mount Pinatubo in the Philippines exploded. The catastrophic volcanic eruption, only some 60 miles from the Philippines capital, Manila, sent more than 17 million tons of sulfur dioxide particles into the atmosphere in the largest volcanic cloud ever measured.

Over the ensuing year, as the ash cloud spread through the stratosphere, climate and atmospheric scientists estimated that Pinatubo's dust caused a decrease of about half a degree Celsius in average global temperatures.

Pinatubo showed one thing very clearly: that particulate matter in the higher atmosphere can reflect heat-producing solar radiation back into space, essentially dimming the sun, resulting in lower temperatures on the surface of our planet.

What might be dubbed the "Pinatubo Effect" is now one part of the global political and scientific debate over how humanity should respond to our worsening, self-made climate emergency.

One side of the debate argues that if volcanoes can cool the planet by sending dust and ash into the upper atmosphere, then surely humans can do the same. Wouldn't it be great if there were a way to recreate the Pinatubo Effect safely by deliberately sending particles into the atmo-

MILA ROSENTHAL *is the Executive Director of the International Science Reserve at the New York Academy of Sciences, where she runs a network of researchers, technologists, and institutions for scientific crisis preparation and response to global climate and health disasters. She co-founded the climate solutions nonprofit Planet Reimagined and teaches climate justice advocacy and human rights campaigning as an Adjunct Professor at Columbia University.*

sphere? That would immediately help the struggle to hold down rising global temperatures that are melting the planet's icecaps, submerging island states and coastal lands, and irreparably damaging the glorious diversity of Earth's ecosystems.

This kind of human-made intervention is a kind of atmospheric geoengineering called **Solar Radiation Modification** (SRM). For non-scientists who have heard of it, SRM might conjure up a dystopian sci-fi future, like the icebound setting of the 2013 movie *Snowpiercer*, played out in a world frozen by an SRM experiment gone very badly wrong. But some scientists and their backers believe it offers humanity a realistic, if partial, potential solution to the climate crisis, and as such demands our immediate attention and substantial investment.

SRM is also of interest to some who are dependent on, or profiting from, extending people's dependence on fossil fuels. That includes fossil fuel-producing nations and global oil, gas and coal companies and investors. From this perspective, if atmospheric intervention can cool the planet, then there is less urgency to end the fossil fuel dependency that is the biggest contributor to global heating through the production of greenhouse gases, most notably carbon dioxide.

Despite the risks, the potential benefits — an apparent technological fix that might help with warming seas and melting ice — mean that SRM research is receiving increased government and private interest and funding since 2020. Philanthropists are interested, and some private sector actors see the potential for profit.

Scientists have taken positions both for and against spending resources on new research. Even among the researchers who think there may be potential, many agree that relevant research is so embryonic and fragmentary that risks cannot even be properly iden-

! Before you read, download the companion **Glossary** that includes definitions, a guide to acronyms and abbreviations used in the article, and other material. Go to **www.fpa.org/great_decisions** and select a topic in the Resources section. (Top right)

> There are currently three basic areas of scientific interest in solar radiation modification and atmospheric geoengineering:
> **Stratospheric Aerosol Injection** (SAI)— This approach seeks to mimic the Mount Pinatubo effect by using airplanes or balloons to disperse particles into the upper atmosphere, which in turn reflect back and diffuse the sun's rays.
> **Marine Cloud Whitening** (MCA)—Operating at much lower levels, MCA seeks to evaporate seawater sprayed from ships to increase particulate salt in stratocumulus clouds over the sea, which already play an important role in reflecting back sunlight.
> **Cirrus Cloud Thinning** (CCT)—While it also involves clouds, CCT seeks to change the structure of high-level alto-cirrus clouds up to 8 miles above the earth's surface. These thin clouds have only a minimal impact on reflecting sunlight, but serve in general to trap heat on the earth's surface by preventing infrared light from dispersing into the higher atmosphere. CCT would, in theory, reduce heat trapping.

tified, let alone calculated. Many also think it is a distraction from scientific research that focuses on the problem of carbon dioxide and other greenhouse gases (GHG) and global heating. What are the responsibilities of scientists and scientific institutions in these debates?

On the policy side, there are huge questions about who is deciding whether to advance SRM research and how it could be monitored or regulated. That includes questions about the role of the private sector and how to manage the risk that bottom-line concerns would drive decisions. For example, would effective technologies be patented or freely available? Will risky technologies be rushed to implementation? These are profound foreign policy questions. While the causes of climate change have been driven most of all by production and consumption in wealthy countries, the impacts and solutions have no borders. The United States cannot patrol its atmospheric borders, and considerations about researching or deploying technologies like SRM are global and multilateral.

The questions at stake in the debate about SRM are central issues at the intersection of science and policy. Making sure that science and policy intersect for the public good is a key role for organizations like mine, the International Science Reserve at the New York Academy of Sciences, where we seek to drive innovative solutions to society's challenges by advancing scientific research, education, and policy.

These challenges especially come to the fore in the climate emergency, as scientific research has been far ahead of policymaking in responses to the existential threat of global heating. That scientific consensus is reflected in regular reports of the Intergovernmental Panel on Climate Change (IPCC). Set up in 1988, the IPCC's scientific assessment reports are based on a survey of the work of thousands of scientists around the world. They have provided the annual COP meetings of the UN Framework Convention on Climate Change with definitive summaries of the state of our efforts to cut emissions and combat global warming.

The most recent IPCC synthesis report on scientific research, produced in March 2023, underlines the gravity of the crisis we are in.

The IPCC warned that we are failing to meet the goals set by the 2015 Paris Climate Agreement for reducing the output of global carbon dioxide, needed to combat rising planetary temperatures. As a result, it looks like we will fail to limit the rise in global temperatures to no more than 1.5 degrees Celsius above preindustrial levels—the scientific estimate for the point at which the effects of climate change become irreversible. In 2022, global temperatures averaged 1.2 degrees Celsius above preindustrial levels.

According to the UN Secretary-General, Antonio Guterres, the 2023 IPCC report documented for the world that rising temperatures showed that the "climate time bomb is ticking....In short," he added, "our world needs climate action on all fronts - everything, everywhere, all at once."

Does "everything" include solar radiation modification? Much remains unknown about how these approaches would work in practice. We don't fully understand their likely impact beyond estimates, which are disputed, of the topline reduction in global heat. And we are nowhere close to addressing the political decisions involved. How, and by whom, should such intervention be authorized and attempted? What happens if India, for example, chooses to launch a Stratospheric Aerosol Injection project that impacts the climate of neighboring Pakistan? What happens if Thailand diverts critical rainfall from Malaysia, or if Korea doubles the amount of winter snow that falls on Japan?

Another volcanic eruption, of Indonesia's Mount Tambora in 1815, reminds us of the risks involved. Tambora was the largest volcanic eruption in recorded history. Its huge dust and ash plume was swept around the planet and damaged agricultural output from China's Yangtze Valley to the farms of northern New England in the United States, causing widespread hardship in what has been dubbed "the year without summer".

Science without regulation

Herbert Boyer (UCSF) and Paul Berg (Stanford) at a conference at Asilomar, February 26, 1975. Berg went on to win a Nobel Prize in chemistry for his work in recombinant DNA.
PETER BREINING/SAN FRANCISCO CHRONICLE/GETTY IMAGES

The grim increase in destructive impacts of climate change, such as intensifying hurricanes and cyclones, and the growing sense of global urgency, if not panic, have led to a steady increase in public interest in ways that solar geoengineering might be used to reverse warming. But the scientific community has long been debating the ethical and political issues that solar geoengineering raises.

Scientists first attempted to agree on how to proceed on this issue in 2010. Over 150 scientists, engineers, lawyers, disaster relief experts and environmentalists met in California's Monterey peninsula for the Asilomar International Conference on Climate Intervention Technologies. Attendees tried to determine how best to reduce the risks associated with experiments on the climate, which most evidently include the risks of unintended consequences.

The choice of Asilomar as the location for this event is, itself, instructive. In 1975, Asilomar hosted another pivotal scientific conference. The scientific community convened to formalize the study, implementation, and future of a rapidly developing area of scientific research that was going to change the way humans live: biotechnology.

The 1975 conference focused on setting safety standards and research principles for genetic experiments involving combining DNA molecules from different species. The meeting was convened by scientists leading the field, though physicians and lawyers also attended. Together they set out to establish what was acceptable scientific endeavor and what was not; in short, scientists were voluntarily agreeing to stop research to assess potential hazards, applying one of the first examples of what is now known as the precautionary principle.

The conference did indeed produce a set of guidelines and restrictions on genetic experiments. But these also had an important, broader, political consequence: by holding a public, open debate on risks, the scientists in attendance helped assuage public anxiety about the new field, which in turn helped preempt any attempt by the government to develop a legal, regulatory framework for future scientific research.

The end result was a voluntary agreement that laid the groundwork for the subsequent development of the leading U.S. biotechnology industry, which transformed medical therapeutics around the world.

Similar concerns were in play at the 2010 Asilomar International Conference on Climate Intervention Technologies. According to one observer's account at the time, the meeting demonstrated (amongst other things) that geoengineering was "a tabula rasa in the public mind," with one survey finding that 74% of respondents knew nothing about it at all.

After an apparently free-ranging, five-day debate that included questions of whether private companies should be able to profit from the new climate interventions, the meeting concluded with a set of principles, the first being that "The core rationale for pursuit of climate engineering research is to advance the collective well-being of society and the environment."

Others included ensuring climate engineering research is internationally planned and coordinated; that it is subject to government oversight with public involvement; and a commitment to "regular, independent evaluation and assessment of the extent of understanding and uncertainty is carried out to provide optimal information and confidence for the public and policymakers."

That same year, climate-related geoengineering was the subject of the first international agreement on the question, one that is still nominally current, but of doubtful weight. In 2010, the 193 members of the UN Convention on Biodiversity agreed that there should be a global moratorium on major geoengineering projects, including not only SRM but also carbon capture. This moratorium was reaffirmed in 2016.

Yet, in the absence of regulatory controls, efforts have been made that violate either the Asilomar ideals or the standards of the Biodiversity Convention. In late 2022, for instance, an American entrepreneur began using hot air balloons to release sulfur particles in the air over Mexico as part of a supposed Stratospheric Aerosol Injection (SAI) cooling experiment. The scheme sought to attract investors to the start-up Make Sunsets; those investors would be given carbon credits in exchange for the balloon launches they funded in Mexico's Baja California, all without any kind of government approval.

Mexico quickly announced a total ban on solar geoengineering experiments in their country.

State of the field

The Make Sunsets escapade was, however, one indicator of a surge of interest in developing solar geoengineering solutions to reverse climate change since the 2010 Asilomar meeting.

Until recently, the U.S. federal government has not been an active funder of research in this field. As a result, researchers turned to philanthropic funding that, in 2018, financed two-thirds of research in the United States. Overall funding has been comparatively low–just over $25 million in North America between 2008 and 2018, which was slightly ahead of investment in Europe.

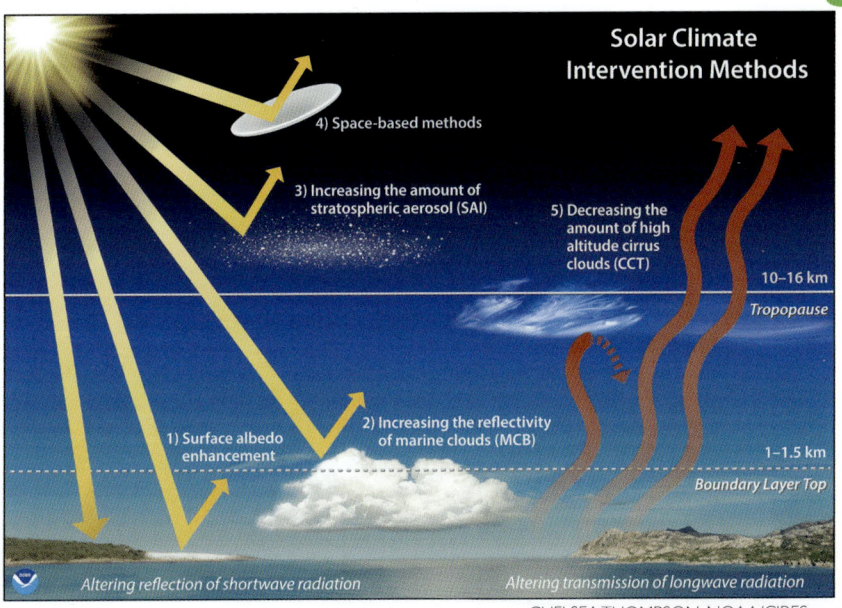

In 2017, for instance, over $7 million was raised from philanthropic US funders (including the William and Flora Hewlett Foundation and Bill Gates) to support the Stratospheric Controlled Perturbation Experiment (SCoPEx) by atmospheric scientists at the Keutsch Research Group, part of the Solar Geoengineering Research Program at Harvard University.

The project, envisaged to cost $20 million, has been the largest U.S. project focused on SRM. It proposed using a stratospheric balloon flying 20km above the earth's surface to assess the global cooling effects of spraying Calcium Carbonate dust (what non-chemists call chalk) into the upper atmosphere to reflect the sun's light.

Other projects across the country have received funding from another private foundation, SilverLining, which says it funds "research and policy efforts on near-term climate risks and interventions such as increasing the reflection of sunlight from clouds and particles in the atmosphere."

Separately, George Soros, who has given over $32 billion away to fund social justice and human rights causes around the world, used a 2023 speech to highlight the Marine Cloud Whitening ideas of David King, the UK's former chief scientific adviser. King has proposed protecting Greenland ice from summer sun by generating clouds from evaporated seawater produced by scores of floating barges deployed around the Arctic coast.

Dr. King also helped create Cambridge University's Centre for Climate Repair, launched in 2019. The center is perhaps the highest profile European scientific research group dedicated to reversing climate change through geoengineering solutions; it also works with the Technical University of Delft Climate Institute (TUDCI) in the Netherlands.

But while funding in the U.S. has until now been mainly sourced from philanthropies, since 2020 there has been a growing government interest, responding at least in part to a report from an important collective voice of the scientific community, the National Academies of Sciences, Engineering and Medicine.

In 2021 the National Academies issued a report, *Reflecting Sunlight: Recommendations for Solar Geoengineering Research and Research Governance*, that called on the federal government to "pursue a research program for solar geoengineering—in coordination with other nations, subject to governance, and alongside a robust portfolio of climate mitigation and adaptation policies." The report includes a thorough overview of

Pipelines at the Gorgon liquefied natural gas (LNG) and carbon capture and storage (CCS) facility, operated by Chevron Corp., on Barrow Island, Australia, on July 24, 2023. Chevron received approval to develop the site into a major LNG export facility on the basis that they could capture and store 80% of the CO2 mixed in with the fuel, instead of releasing it. LISA MAREE WILLIAMS/BLOOMBERG/GETTY IMAGES

the current thinking about what further work would need to be done to assess the impacts of solar geoengineering. It recommended the government spend between $100–200 million on solar geoengineering research over the coming five years. The report also estimated that delivering a 1% drop in global temperatures using high altitude SAI techniques might cost more than $15 billion annually, noting that "These costs are small compared to the costs of climate change but large enough to be out of reach for some potential actors."

Following the National Academies, in 2022 the White House Office of Science and Technology Policy (OSTP) began coordinating a five-year research plan into a "scientific assessment of solar and other rapid climate interventions in the context of near-term climate risks and hazards." In July 2023, the OSTP published a mandated report to Congress on its current thinking around the research plan.

Pushback: moral hazard

Yet at the same time as we have seen a surge of investment and interest into SRM research, the debate over SRM has expanded significantly, moving beyond the limiting principles established at Asilomar in 2010 to the larger question of whether scientists should be pursuing this approach at all.

In announcing its new funding initiative, for instance, the White House OSTP asserted that research on climate geoengineering was being "handicapped" by intense debates over the "moral hazard" of the issue. Moral hazard, in this case, refers to the argument that geoengineering is a distraction from the more politically difficult challenge of reducing carbon dioxide emissions from fossil fuels and agriculture. According to this argument, we have a very narrow window of opportunity to cut emissions and systemically change the way human societies and economies function. Our attention cannot get diverted by these easy "techno fixes."

Similar arguments have been advanced against proposals to expand research and investment into large-scale high-tech "carbon capture" projects in high-income countries, which seek to take carbon dioxide produced by human activity out of the atmosphere. Fossil fuel corporations and national producers are enthusiastic promoters of carbon capture, which allows for the continued burning of their products, and goes back into extracting new oil, despite the hotly debated question of whether carbon capture can be deployed at scale.

Similar pushback has been aimed at SRM. David Keith, a pioneering researcher in the field of SRM now heading a new Climate Systems Engineering Initiative at the University of Chicago, raised the issue of moral hazard and geoengineering in a paper published in 2000. He wrote: "Knowledge of geoengineering has been characterized as an insurance strategy; in analogy with the moral hazard posed by collective insurance schemes, which encourage behavior that is individually advantageous but not socially optimal, we may ascribe an analogous hazard to geoengineering if it encourages suboptimal investment in mitigation."

In short, if you know you can use geoengineering to reduce the carbon dioxide (CO_2) that drives global warming, then why bother facing the enormous challenge of giving up fossil fuels?

Dr. Keith's 2000 paper suggests that this issue has been dissuading scientists from including geoengineering options in their debates on the climate. Prophetically, he also postulates that "two or three decades hence," the promise of effective geoengineering intervention could undermine the political will to push through a global agreement on costly cuts in CO_2 production. That future is now.

Reflecting these concerns, the National Academies' 2021 report advocating for a federal research program also noted "that those with vested interests in fossil fuels might seize on the prospect of geoengineering as a 'solution' to climate change to support their interests, even if researchers and governments do not promote this framing."

Their report stressed that federal research should focus on building knowledge rather than aiming at deployment, and that it should represent only a minor part of overall federal climate research efforts.

This moral hazard argument was deployed politically to great effect in 2021 against the Harvard SCoPEx experiment (mentioned earlier) that examined the impact of a Stratospheric Aerosol Injection project. Sweden's Esrange rocket range and space research center, located north of the Arctic Circle, was due to test launch SCoPEx's ex-

RISKY SCIENCE ACROSS BORDERS

perimental balloon platform (without the experiment). But representatives of the local indigenous Sami people and environmental activists objected. In an open letter, the critics argued that the experiment would "threaten the reputation and credibility of the climate leadership Sweden wants and must pursue as the only way to deal effectively with the climate crisis: powerful measures for a rapid and just transition to zero emission societies, 100% renewable energy and shutdown of the fossil fuel industry."

As a result of the protests, the Swedish space center decided not to proceed with the launch. In response, the Keutsch Group said the experiment was on hold until a "more thorough societal engagement process can be conducted to address issues related to solar geoengineering research in Sweden."

This background explains why the 2023 White House report to Congress stressed so categorically that its support for research did not represent a change of policy away from reducing carbon emissions. The second paragraph of the report: "Immediate, sustained, and effective reductions of global greenhouse gas emissions are required to slow the pace of climate change and reduce the risk of crossing critical and potentially catastrophic thresholds in the global climate system." Developing a federal research program into solar geoengineering options is secondary to developing carbon capture and sequestration technologies. Research into SRM is primarily aimed "to better understand both the potential benefits and risks".

The White House also maintained the cautious "do no harm" approach outlined in the National Academies' *Reflecting Sunlight* report, including a caution "that any potential comprehensive research program must encompass the societal as well as the scientific dimensions of solar radiation modification." It highlighted three priority objectives:
■ Determining climate and environmental impacts of solar radiation modification deployment
■ Assessing potential societal outcomes and ecological consequences
■ Examining how research might be done in cooperation among international partners

Pushback: humanitarian hazard

Other arguments, too, fuel opposition to SRM experiments. There is a serious and widespread debate among scientists about whether the technology is even effective, or, possibly, simply too dangerous.

In 2017, a group of British scientists from the UK's Met Office Hadley Centre for Climate Science published a paper in the journal *Nature*, arguing that moves to use SAI sulfate dispersal could go spectacularly wrong.

They based their conclusions on a study that showed the impact of volcanic eruptions in the northern hemisphere in Alaska in 1912 and at El Chichón in Mexico in 1982. Those eruptions could be linked to droughts that followed in Africa's Sahel region.

They then used their climate models to simulate what might happen if sulfate particles were injected into the stratosphere in SAI interventions. If such a project injected five million tons of sulfate into the upper atmosphere over the northern hemisphere every year between 2020 and 2070, they concluded the result would be severe droughts and an almost total loss of vegetation in areas including Sudan, Chad, Senegal, Mali, and Niger. Doing the same in the southern hemisphere, the study concluded, would benefit the Sahel with Increased rains, but drastically cut rainfall in north-eastern Brazil.

Underlining these concerns are more fundamental questions about the accuracy of climate computer modeling at a local level. For example, Kate Marvel, a scientist specializing in climate modeling at Project Drawdown, explained the problem at an October 2023 public event, Reflecting Risk: Rights-Based Global Decision-Making about Research and Testing of Solar Geoengineering Climate Tech, hosted by the International Science Reserve at the New York Academy of Sciences. Existing computer models could predict top level changes that might result from solar reflection interventions. But, she argued, that they could not track the local impacts of what that would mean for rainfall.

"We will never be able to say that this particular level of stratospheric aerosol injection will certainly cause this particular impact in this particular locality. We are just never going to be able to have that certainty in an extremely complex system."

Dr. Marvel went on to raise that

On the first night of Climate Week NYC, on September 18, 1923, and ahead of the Climate Ambition Summit in New York City, the Adler Hall at The New York Society for Ethical Culture hosted an array of climate communicators, including climate scientist Dr. Kate Marvel, gathering in conversation at Up2Us2023: A Better World is Possible. ERIK MCGREGOR/LIGHTROCKET/GETTY IMAGES

"third category" of possible impacts, "the unknown unknowns, that for me is the really, really frightening category, because those are the questions that we have not even thought to ask."

The challenges of assessing the global impact of changes in the atmosphere resulting from human activity have been demonstrated recently by one real world example, although one that involves not adding, but taking sulfates out of the atmosphere.

In 2020, the International Maritime Organization, a UN body whose primary focus is regulating world shipping and combating pollution of the seas, adopted its "IMO 2020" regulation to drastically reduce emissions of sulfur oxide (SOx) from global shipping, produced by burning sulfur-heavy fuel oils. This action is aimed at reducing acid rain and improving air quality.

Initial studies concluded that the new regulations have, as hoped, significantly reduced SOx emissions. However, they also thinned high-level particle clouds over shipping lanes, clouds which reduce the heating effect of the sun on the ocean. An analysis by *Carbon Brief* estimated that that the likely side-effect of the SOx reduction will be to increase global temperatures by around 0.05C by 2050, the equivalent of two years of current global emissions.

Carbon Brief also noted that some researchers have proposed a link between the reduced air pollution and a spike in temperatures in the Atlantic, a theory that gained significant public attention amid extreme summer weather in parts of northern Europe.

Beyond that, on social media, advocates of geoengineering began arguing that the rise in sea temperatures was directly attributable to the reduction in aerosol sulfates in the atmosphere. This led to the conclusion that in effect, we had already been altering our atmosphere through inadvertent Solar Radiation Modification, so why not do it in earnest?

@HankGreen, a video blogger with an X-account that has 1.6 million followers, posted in a thread on August 4: "And the biggest perspective shift for me here is...we shouldn't be asking whether we should be doing geoengineering...we already are, we have been for a century. We should be asking... should take a huge step and do it intentionally and thoughtfully...because WE CAN SEE IT WORKS."

But *Carbon Brief* also noted that other factors complicate efforts to explain the spike in ocean temperatures attributed to shipping regulations; those factors include: an underwater eruption in the South Pacific; an unusual reduction in dust from the Sahara; the Canadian summer wildfires that darkened skies over the northeast of the United States; and the onset of the El Niño weather pattern.

In short, the scientific jury is still out on the impact of the reduction in smoke particles from container ships crossing the world's shipping lanes.

In one other recent development, a group of scientists centered on the Max Planck Institute for Chemistry in Germany have questioned assumptions about the cooling impact of SAI using sulfate particles, arguing they may be over-optimistic.

The heated discussions about SAI contrast with the more subdued public anxiety surrounding Marine Cloud Brightening (MCB) experiments. It is notable that in March 2020, Australian scientists carried out an MCB pilot test over areas of the Great Barrier Reef to counter bleaching of the reef's coral attributed to higher seawater temperatures. The experiment, dispersed a mist of salt water over the reef at low levels, attracted minimal public attention. Scientists from the Australian Forum for Climate Intervention Governance (AFCIG) suggesting a number of factors to explain the lack of reaction, including broad public familiarity with cloud seeding technologies to create rain and the concurrent, catastrophic wildfires raging in the southeast of the country.

In contrast, a British government-backed experiment using hoses suspended from high altitude balloons to spray cloud-brightening droplets (known as Stratospheric Particle Injection for Climate Engineering, or SPICE) was canceled in 2012, following a fight over private patents that reflected broader opposition from some in the scientific community.

Foreign policy and international regulation

Taken together, the current surge of both interest in, and backlash to, Solar Radiation Modification raises a central question: who is in charge?

The White House, for instance, may be keen to advance further research into Solar Radiation Modification geoengineering's viability. But given that atmospheric interventions have global implications, it is vital to consider how the White House will act when it makes a decision regarding SRM.

There are also broader geopolitical factors beyond the science to consider. Patrycja Sasnal, a Polish political scientist and diplomat, led work on a recent report to the UN Human Rights Council on the human rights implications of new climate technologies. She noted at the New York Academy of Sciences' 2023 "Reflecting Risk" event that dependency on dispersing particulate matter in the upper atmosphere would have a huge impact on global power structures. In particular, she noted the implications of the need to maintain and replenish a "sunscreen" in the upper atmosphere to avoid the predicted heat spike that scientists predict would follow suspension of the system.

According to Sasnal, this "can cause or engender a new political system, like the nuclear weapons have, because once this technology had started and it started at scale, it has to be continued. Or if it is phased out, it would have to be phased out very gradually. But we've put an obligation on future generations, and because of its transboundary effects, it would cause political conflict for sure."

In its 2023 report to Congress, the White House OSTP stressed the need for international cooperation on research on what is clearly a cross-border issue. It notes laconically that "an unexpected SRM deployment might incur significant geopolitical outcomes" and that "a lack of country-level dialogue, governance bodies, and research norms might increase the possibility that state or non-state actors could move independently to develop and deploy SRM technologies."

But these optimal, or even sub-optimal, international frameworks do not yet exist, or exist only in a piecemeal fashion. For instance, the International Maritime Organization decided in October 2023 to include Marine Cloud Brightening in a review of the impact of four marine geoengineering techniques, urging that reviewers assess potential risks with the "utmost caution."

Meanwhile, 2023 saw another high-level effort to take stock of the implications of missing the Paris Agreement emission reduction targets, by another initiative: the independent Global Commission on Governing Risks from Climate Overshoot, a group of 12 leading international figures, convened with the support of the French government and other funders, tasked with examining options for action that went "beyond emissions reduction."

The Climate Overshoot Commission notes that it is the first independent international body to look at the implications of failing to hold the rise in world temperatures to below 1.5 degrees Celsius.

Its report, published in September 2023, stresses the urgent need to cut carbon emissions and for the high-income countries to fund climate adaptation and energy transition in low- and middle- income countries. And, as the last of its ten recommendations, it calls for a moratorium on the deployment of solar radiation modification and large-scale experiments "when they pose a risk of significant transboundary harm, whilst supporting internationally inclusive research into and assessment of its future potential."

The report adds that SRM "is a high stakes, global impacts, and deep uncertainties approach" and that countries should adopt a moratorium without waiting for a formal, legally binding treaty. The calls for a moratorium and negotiations on a treaty represent a mainstream view of the role of multilateral diplomacy in science and technology. But the challenges to the approach are manifold. In addition to the complexities of the issue itself, the erosion of multilateral cooperation in the aftermath of Russia's invasion of Ukraine and other geopolitical factors, such as growing tensions between the United States and China, have significantly diminished the prospects for effective government-to-government agreement on this or other issues.

The principles established at the Asilomar Conference on climate geoengineering back in 2010 might remain a good place to start, including the principle that the debate over geoengineering needs to be public and open to all those affected. That clearly must include the policymakers and scientists of low- and middle-income countries.

The report presented to the UN Human Rights Council on the human rights impacts of climate geoengineering concluded that "states should adopt and implement restrictive regulations on solar radiation modification experiments, where necessary, including a ban on outdoor experiments, while only allowing conditional and controlled research." The report added that "the lack of a mechanism to prevent the development of harmful solar radiation modification techniques should be addressed in a manner that includes the global South and climate vulnerable States and communities."

Some very limited efforts have ostensibly been made. Open Philanthropy—one of the funders of the Harvard SCoPEx SAI project—announced in January 2023 that it was giving $900,000 to the Degrees Initiative, a non-profit group dedicated to giving developing countries' scientists a voice in global debates on SRM.

But there is a high level of distrust in countries of the Global South, even about efforts such as the Degrees Initiative that are ostensibly aimed at including more voices in a debate on SRM.

Writing in the *New York Times* in April, 2023, in an opinion piece headlined "My Continent is Not Your Geoengineering Laboratory," Chukwumerije Okereke, a Nigerian climate scientist, expressed support for the call for a moratorium on climate geoengineering, suggesting that groups such as the Degrees Initiative were trying to "entice" African governments into supporting geoengineering projects.

Talk of putting "developing countries at the center" of the geoengineering debate, he wrote, "just appears to be a way of trying to make Africa a test case for an unproven technology. Indeed more studies into this hypothetical solution look like steps toward development and a slippery slope to eventual deployment."

Is there a way forward for global regulation?

The Council on Energy, Environment, and Water (CEEE), a New Delhi-based think tank and policy institution, has proposed that there is already a viable candidate to take on the role of overseeing Solar Geoengineering: the scientific panel that currently monitors the state of the earth's ozone layer.

Over the past 35 years, the Scientific Assessment Panel to the Montreal Protocol on Ozone Depleting Substances has issued reports every four years assessing the impact of the 1987 agreement to eliminate the production of harmful chemicals. Its 2023 report included a chapter looking at the possible impact on the ozone of Stratospheric Aerosol Injection (SAI) in particular, concluding that SAI "could also affect stratospheric temperatures, circulation and ozone production and destruction rates and transport."

The CEEE argues that the Montreal Protocol provides the most serviceable immediate option for establishing a governance structure for SAI, while also urging the creation of an "independent and overarching framework for SRM governance."

The IPCC also assesses the possible impact of solar geoengineering and carbon capture technologies. However, though it can assess the state of the science and the potential impacts of both

Sun sets in the village of Balnoi along the India-Pakistan border in Mendhar, Poonch District, India, on Friday, on June 9th, 2023. NAZIM ALI KHAN/NURPHOTO/GETTY IMAGES

solar radiation management and carbon capture, the IPCC is not designed to monitor or regulate.

In the absence of any formal, multilateral forum that is focused on the issues, the Independent Climate Overshoot Committee supports in the interim what might be considered a science diplomacy solution. It argues that governments, while maintaining a moratorium on "large-scale" experiments, should "expand scientific research and pursue international dialogues on how to govern [atmospheric geoengineering] effectively, prudently, and justly."

This science diplomacy approach can be developed even without governments. For example, the AGU, a U.S.-based earth sciences organization with over 130,000 members globally, and the world's largest grouping of climate researchers, announced in 2022 its intention develop an "ethical framework to guide the research and possible deployment of climate change intervention measures".

AGU sought to launch discussions around such a framework on the sidelines of the COP27 Climate Summit in Egypt in 2022. While it did not take a position on specific climate interventions, carefully hedging its planned framework in deference to the global sensitivities, the organization ultimately said that geoengineering is not a substitute for "aggressive action" to reduce carbon dioxide emissions.

AGU President Susan Lozier said the objective would be to "look at how the scientific community approached research around genetic engineering and human participation in health, medical, and social science research." She made the explicit comparison to other dilemmas in research and policy: "Prior global gatherings, such as the 2010 Asilomar Conference on Climate Engineering, as well as lessons from biomedical research, have already established strong starting principles for this work."

But even talking about an ethical framework is a step too far for those who argue that geoengineering solutions are a wasteful distraction. At COP27 in Egypt, the notion of advancing a research framework on Solar Modification remained on the sidelines.

For communities at immediate risk from the climate crisis, notably in poorer countries, the issue is regarded as largely irrelevant. The declaration issued at the end of the Africa Climate Summit in Nairobi in September 2023, setting out the African Union's position ahead of the COP28 meeting in the UAE, made no mention of geoengineering. It was dominated instead by concerns over climate and development financing, including how to pay for transitions away from dependence on fossil fuels, as well as funding for loss and damage resulting from climate damage caused by wealthy countries' emissions.

Within the scientific community as well, some are deeply opposed to current exploration of the issues around SRM. In spring of 2023, hundreds of scientists and others joined a call for an International Solar Engineering Non-Use Agreement, which would take geoengineering off the agenda altogether.

Meanwhile, without the basic elements of governance in place, some philanthropic funders and investors seem eager to push ahead, driven by their belief that the crisis demands urgent action. Of the three SRM approaches, MCB seems the most likely to become a reality at scale, despite the IMO's review.

In one sign of the new urgency around the issue, the University of Cambridge and its partner in Delft received funding in early 2023 for its MCB work from the Refreeze the Arctic Foundation. The foundation was launched just a year earlier by the heirs of a Dutch businessman-turned-philanthropist. The foundation has ambitious plans to "fast-track" funding into MCB, with a timeline that envisages "full demonstration facilities" by the end of 2027.

RAF insists that this work must be accompanied by the reduction of carbon dioxide emissions to almost nothing. But it is clear about its mission: "We will begin by refreezing targeted areas, before implementing this at a much larger scale. Eventually, this will lead to refreezing the Arctic."

Patrycja Sasnal, who led the group that produced the report to the UN Human Rights Council on climate engineering, takes a more nuanced approach, arguing that maybe one day discussions on considering SRM will be needed, but not yet.

"Solar geoengineering is not the solution for now," she said at the "Reflecting Risk" event. "Maybe it will be sometime in the future. But for now, many believe we cannot even afford to spend the resources of our thinking, money, or time on this topic."

RISKY SCIENCE ACROSS BORDERS

Discussion questions:

1. Should there be a global moratorium on SRM research and should its use be prohibited?

2. The Intergovernmental Panel on Climate Change (IPCC) has placed science at the heart of global negotiations around the climate crisis. But scientists are not the lead decision-makers, and powerful actors like governments and industries don't follow the science. Should scientists have more power in global decision-making? How would that work?

3. How might there be an informed debate around SRM and its potential for lowering global temperatures without undermining the urgent need to cut carbon dioxide emissions?

4. What should be the role of the private sector in scientific and technological research and development to address climate change? Are there benefits and/or risks of private investment versus government funding in supporting experimentation and deployment of Solar Radiation Management systems?

5. What might be some of the geopolitical effects if there were transnational damage caused by SRM deployment, such as crop failures or rainfall pattern changes?

6. How might long-term deployment of SAI, requiring regular replenishment of particulate matter in the upper atmosphere, change dynamics of global politics?

7. What elements would be required for an effective global governance system on SRM?

Suggested readings

Carnegie Climate Governance Institute, 2023. "Global status of activities relating to Solar Radiation Modification and its governance." Ninth Edition. September 14, 2023. Briefing note by the Carnegie Climate Governance Initiative summarizing key insights into activities relating to solar radiation modification and its governance globally

Climate Overshoot Commission, 2023. Chapter 8. Solar Radiation Modification. Pg. 86–94, This article is a recent, high-level overview of the scientific and governance challenges and potential opportunities associated with solar radiation modification. It is one chapter in a larger report by the Climate Overshoot Commission on reducing emissions to meet climate targets.

Felgenhauer, Tyler et al., 2022. "Solar Radiation Modification: A Risk-Risk Analysis." Carnegie Climate Governance Initiative. In this paper, a risk-risk tradeoff framework is used to compare a world with SRM and a world without SRM in addressing climate change.

National Academies of Sciences, Engineering, and Medicine, 2021. "Reflecting Sunlight: Recommendations for Solar Geoengineering Research and Research Governance." The National Academies Press

Suarez, Pablo and Maarten K. van Aalst. "Geoengineering: A humanitarian concern." This paper explores the humanitarian dimensions of geoengineering, specifically relating to solar radiation management (SRM), drawing from the engagement of the Red Cross Red Crescent Climate Centre in SRM discussions, discussing how to improve linkages between science, policy and humanitarian practice.

United Nations Environment Program (UNEP), February 2023 One Atmosphere: An Independent Expert Review on Solar Radiation Modification Research and Deployment. This report by the UNEP finds that SRM is not yet ready for large-scale deployment to cool the Earth. The Panel says it is no substitute for a rapid reduction in greenhouse gas emissions, which must remain the global priority.

United Nations Human Rights Council (UNHRC), September 2023. Impact of new technologies for climate protection on the enjoyment of human rights. UN Human Rights Council Advisory Committee report, including inputs from the Special Rapporteur on the promotion and protection of human rights in the context of climate change.

U.S. Office of Science and Technology Policy (OSTP). 2023. Congressionally Mandated Research Plan and an Initial Research Governance: Framework Related to Solar Radiation Modification. The report, which was developed in coordination with the National Oceanic and Atmospheric Administration and other key federal agencies, identifies critical knowledge gaps and scopes potential research areas that could improve understanding of risks and benefits posed by solar radiation modification.

Don't forget to vote!
Download a copy of the ballot questions from the Resources page at www.fpa.org/great_decisions

---

To access web links to these readings, as well as links to additional, shorter readings and suggested web sites,
GO TO **www.fpa.org/great_decisions**
and click on the topic under Resources, on the right-hand side of the page.

4

Technology denial and Sino-American rivalry
by Jonathan Chanis

President Richard Nixon during the historic 1972 trip to China that began the normalization of U.S.-China relations; He is shown above with Chinese Premier Chou En-Lai greeting a young girl in Hangzhou, China. RICHARD NIXON MUSEUM AND LIBRARY

America and the world were stunned in 1972 when U.S. President Richard Nixon, an unwavering anti-communist, traveled to China and ended decades of bitter hostility between the United States and China. During the decade before the trip, the Soviet Union had largely closed the military gap between the two superpowers, and the China opening helped the United States redress its deteriorating geopolitical position. By the 1980s, to balance growing Soviet power, the United States even sold military equipment to China. While these sales largely ended after the Chinese 1989 Tiananmen Square crackdown, the Sino-American relationship continued to improve as China liberalized its economy and integrated into the U.S.-dominated international trading system. The goodwill between the two states, however, began to decline after General Secretary Xi Jinping came to power in 2012 and China began to challenge American interests in east Asia.

Today, the United States and China are rivals and the relationship is marked by numerous conflicts such as Chi-

JONATHAN CHANIS *has worked in investment management, emerging markets finance, and commodities trading for over 25 years. Currently he manages New Tide Asset Management, a company focused on global and resource trading. He previously worked at Citigroup and Caxton Associates where he traded energy and emerging market equities, and commodities and currencies. He has taught undergraduate and graduate courses on political economy, public policy, international politics, and other subjects at several education institutions including Columbia University.*

nese efforts to unify with Taiwan by force if necessary; claims on the South China Sea; support for North Korea and its nuclear program; suppression of democracy in Hong Kong; human rights abuses in Xinjiang; and a turn toward mercantilist economic policies channeling growing economic power into military power. While the United States, especially under the Biden administration, continues to search for a mutual accommodation of U.S. and Chinese interests, the overall U.S. policy toward China has turned adversarial.

The primary motive for this anti-China, "new Washington consensus" is the change in the military balance. America's relative military position declined precipitously over the last decade and there is a distressing realization that the existing U.S. force structure and military equipment acquisition procedures are ill-suited for dealing with the rapidly growing Chinese military challenge. The policy change also stems from America's deteriorating economic competitiveness. While China's economic rise lowered import prices and increased American purchasing power, it also unemployed approximately 2.4 million Americans between 1991 and 2011. This represents almost half of all manufacturing jobs lost during that period.

Since there are fewer U.S. manufacturing workers left to displace, the negative employment impact of China's economic policies on U.S. manufacturing has decreased, but many now see China's current economic policies as even more dangerous. Robert Atkinson, of the Information Technology and Information Foundation, argues that China's "...actions are part of a coordinated campaign of mercantilist aggression to capture global leadership in advanced industries by stealing technology from rivals and propping up its state champions with massive subsidies, among other measures..."

! Before you read, download the companion **Glossary** that includes definitions, a guide to acronyms and abbreviations used in the article, and other material. Go to **www.fpa.org/great_decisions** and select a topic in the Resources section. (Top right)

While support for the new, anti-China "consensus" based on economic concerns is less widespread than support based on America's declining military position, both concerns incentivize some policymakers to seek to deny China access to U.S. technology and investment, especially those involving semiconductors. Semiconductors are electric components used in products such as memory chips, microprocessor, and integrated circuits. They are ubiquitous in modern life. Many view the world's semiconductors dependency as equivalent to the 20th century's oil and gas dependency. Semiconductors are the ultimate foundational technology in a rapidly digitalizing world.

A technology denial strategy is seen both as a logical and necessary corrective to decades of increasingly predatory Chinese economic policies, as well as a way to slow down China military modernization and provide time for the U.S. military to correct known deficiencies. Consequently, the Biden administration has not only continued Trump administration technology restrictions, it has tightened semiconductors export controls and limited the transfer of semiconductor manufacturing equipment to China. More contentiously, it is seeking to restrict outbound U.S. technology investment to China.

The current and emerging U.S. technology and investment restrictions are akin to a limited 19th century economic naval blockade. They are designed to undermine China's ability to project power by limiting or destroying the resources necessary for pursuing military, if not economic, expansion. A technology denial strategy is attractive because it is non-violent, and many of the actions necessary for its execution can be taken unilaterally. To detractors, however, the strategy goes beyond the administration's stated military and economic concerns and constitutes "containment." It is seen as provocative, unwarranted, and counterproductive.

Many progressives view hostility toward China as unjustified given the U.S.' own "imperial" policies, and as "fear-mongering" to distract Americans from the sources of, and solutions for, their problems. More mainstream Democrats and Republicans view pursuing a China technology denial strategy as endangering American welfare by reversing decades of gains made through trade with, and investment in, China. The American and Chinese economies are deeply integrated; they are "coupled" in ways that create multiple, and occasionally even unknown, interdependences. Radically altering this relationship through escalating economic warfare is risky and could be extremely costly. However, it is undeniable that China has benefitted immensely from its economic relationship with the United States and that this economic relationship and accompanying technology transfer and investment have allowed China to place long-held American interests at risk. Facilitating China's continued economic development through unrestrained technology trade and investment may further undermine U.S. security, and potentially even prosperity. As U.S. Representative Mike Gallagher, the Chairman of the House Select Committee on the Strategic Competition Between the United States and the Chinese Communist Party (CCP) said, "We shouldn't be funding our own destruction."

On the surface, there appears to be a solid "consensus" for getting economically "tough on China," but this policy is deeply, and often quietly, contested. While many congressional members vocalize strong support for tough China action, their voting records often indicate otherwise. Efforts to slow down or stop tougher China policies are supported by many Democratic members with technology industry ties; "traditional pro-business" Republicans; Democratic progressives; and the isolationist wing of the Republican Freedom Caucus. On the other side are Democratic and Republican "China Hawks," and industrial policy Democrats, and "new conservative" Republicans concerned with China's predatory economic actions.

Within the Biden administration and federal government, there are large policy differences, especially between the Department of Defense (DoD), and the Treasury and Commerce Departments. The problem is that U.S. policy cannot decide whether China is a national security threat or a business opportunity. It is conceivable that China is both, and in many respects, this represents the Biden Administration's current policy. However, this makes forming coherent policy extremely difficult. The set of policies required if China is a national security threat are antithetical to those that treat China as a business opportunity. In order to better understand this dilemma, this essay will: 1) assess the economic relationship and the role of investment and technology in the rivalry; 2) explain why technology policy has become so dominant in the rivalry; 3) delineate the current status of U.S. semiconductor and investment restrictions; and 4) review the arguments for and against these restrictions.

Economic relations, investment and technology

Over the last 30 years, China has accomplished one of the most miraculous economic transformations in history. Its economy grew at over 9% per year, and it became the world's second largest economy and largest manufacturer and exporter. China's share of global exports rose from under 5% in 2000 to almost 20% in 2022. (See Figure 1.) It took 500 million people out of abject poverty and changed from a rural, agricultural society into an advanced technological one. China accomplished this miraculous transformation by continually experimenting with different forms of economic organization. It was, in a phrase later used by Deng Xiaoping, like "crossing the river by feeling the stones."

Beginning in 1977, China embarked on a series of reforms by ending Soviet style economic planning, integrating markets into Chinese society, and entering more fully into the global economy. It de-collectivized agriculture; eliminated price controls on a range of industrial and agricultural products; encouraged citizens to start their own businesses; and attracted foreign direct investment (FDI). Attracting FDI, a type of investment where the investor has control over the enterprise's operations, was central to China's economic reforms.

To attract FDI, China created over a dozen "special economic zones" (SEZs) that provided foreign companies with more profitable operating conditions. This included tax concessions, free or discounted land, and reduced utility charges. In addition to the SEZs, China also lowered labor costs by allowing hundreds of millions of peasants to move from the countryside to cities to work in export-oriented factories. Substantially lower labor costs and a market with a billion potential consumers were not the only reasons companies flocked to China. As Clyde Prestowitz, a trade advisor to four U.S. presidents wrote: U.S. corporations were equally interested in "... circumventing labor unions, environmental restrictions, and liability for any factory mishaps [and] then because of favorable U.S. trade treatment...exporting back to the United States and other developed...markets."

As a result of both Chinese governmental policies and market pressure for companies to maximize profits, foreign direct investment in China surged. Starting from almost zero at the end of the 1970s, it reached $40–$45 billion per year in the second half of the 1990s. After China's admission to the WTO in 2001, FDI doubled in less than 10 years (See Figure 2). By 2010, there were over 445,000 foreign invested enterprises (FIEs) employing over 55 million workers, or almost 16% of the urban Chinese labor force.

Between 2009 and 2019, U.S. investment into China ranged from $13–16 billion per year, and the cumulative

Fig. 2: Foreign Direct Investment into China (in Millions USD)

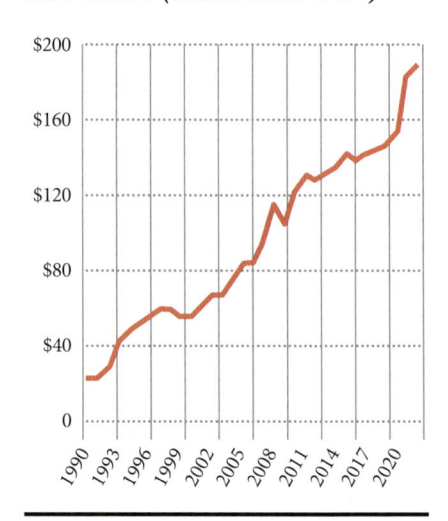

SOURCE: UNCTAD. World Investment Report, 2023.

Fig. 1: China Share of World Exports After 2001 WTO Entry

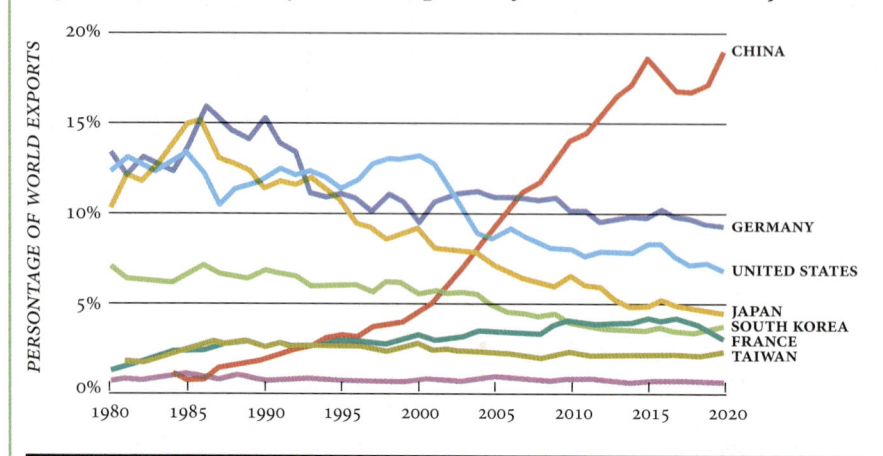

SOURCE: World Bank, Manufacturing exports; Taiwan Ministry of Finance, exports, www.ceicdata.com/en

value of U.S. investment from 1990 through early 2020 exceeded $250 billon. Over the decades, the sectors receiving this investment moved from labor intensive export manufacturing to domestic Chinese consumer-oriented industries, and now to technology which constitutes over $40 billion of total investment.

The contribution of foreign investment and foreign enterprises to China's economic success cannot be underestimated. According to an International Monetary Fund (IMF) study, foreign investment and foreign enterprises raised total Chinese investment, increased productivity and employment, and created the dynamic export sector. The IMF estimated that FDI contributed nearly three percentage points, or approximately a quarter to one third, to China's annual GDP growth during these early years. And this contribution was not simply the result of access to foreign capital. More significant were positive "spillover effects" between the FIEs and local firms. FIEs tended to be more dynamic and productive than local firms, and local Chinese firms benefited from the introduction of new management skills and better technology and production techniques.

Mercantilism, military-civil fusion, and China's military buildup

Despite opening to foreign capital and reliance on markets in selected sectors, the Chinese state's guiding hand never entirely disappeared. As noted, in the 1980s and most of the 1990s, the Chinese government relied heavily on direct economic intervention. This changed in the years right before and after its WTO accession, when there was minimal direct economic intervention. However, even then, the central and provincial governments retained a degree of control over economic life through government budgets, preferred access to land and credit, and selective prosecutions for corruption. But this more liberal phase of "socialism with Chinese characteristics" was brief.

University of California Professor Barry Naughton and others have observed that in 2006, and especially after the 2008 Global Financial Crisis, China began backtracking on market liberalization. This mercantilist resurgence was primarily directed toward strengthening the technology sector through industrial policies. A primary tool was, and remains, "government guidance funds" (GGFs) that invest in selected companies. By 2022, researchers counted over 2,000 such funds seeking to invest over 12 trillion renminbi (~$1.6 trillion). The largest of these funds are controlled by the China Integrated Circuit Industry Investment Fund, aka "the Big Fund." Its first and second round of funding occurred in 2014 and 2019, and it is now undertaking a third fundraising. Once this third-round finishes, it will have raised close to $100 billion for investment for semiconductor development.

Additional industrial policies include: the use of the state-controlled banking system to funnel capital to favored sectors and companies; the forced sale of "golden shares" to the government, allowing it to intervene in company operations; and embedding political guidance personnel, i.e., CCP members, in local, and increasingly foreign, companies.

Another area of concern for American policymakers is China's "Military-Civil Fusion" (MCF) activities. The U.S. government defines MCF as "the elimination of barriers between China's civilian research and commercial sectors, and its military and defense industrial sectors." MCF was codified in a special five-year plan in 2016, and its goal is to "…systematically reorganize the Chinese science and technology enterprise to ensure that new innovations simultaneously advance economic and military development." According to the U.S. government, the critical technologies targeted by MCF include quantum computing, big data, semiconductors, 5G, advanced nuclear technology, aerospace technology, and AI. Since they are easier to acquire, the strategy is particularly focused on obtaining "dual use" technology, i.e., technologies with civilian and military applications.

MCF uses a wide range of strategies to gain an edge in the technological rivalry, including directly investing in Chinese technology companies or directing them to invest in foreign corporations without disclosing the relationship to China's military; directing academic and research collaboration (including with foreigners) for military gain, forced technology transfer, and intellectual property theft by non-governmental Chinese individuals and companies.

One of the more notable MCF cases involved Beijing Highlander Digital Technology (BHDT), a marine navigation and communications equipment supplier. BHDT used its private sector status to acquire sensitive military technology reportedly now used in China's first locally produced aircraft carrier. It also purchased a Canadian company that worked for the U.S. Navy and transferred sensitive technical information on a submarine rescue system to the People's Liberation Army-Navy (PLAN). BHDT was placed on the U.S. Entity List in 2022 and its ability to interact with U.S. and western companies was constrained, but every private Chinese technology company is now a potential BHDT. According to the State Department, MCF means that "it is very difficult and, in many cases, impossible to engage with China's high-technology sector in a way that does not entangle a foreign entity in supporting ongoing Chinese efforts to develop or otherwise acquire cutting-edge technological capacities for China's armed forces."

As a result of China's rapid economic growth, state-directed focus on technology development, and use of military-civil fusion, China has become a formidable military competitor to the United States. Numerically, the PLAN has the world's largest navy

Xi Jinping inspects People's Liberation Army (PLA) troops during a parade on July 30, 2017, commemorating the 90th anniversary of the PLA's founding. IMAGO/ALAMY STOCK PHOTO

with approximately 340 ships, including 125 major surface combatants. Between the PLAN and People's Liberation Army-Air Force, China has the world's third largest air force, with over 2,800 aircraft. It is investing in, and rapidly modernizing, its land-, sea-, and air-based nuclear platforms, and it has developed both significant information warfare and space/counter space capabilities.

China has committed to completing its military modernization based on "informatization, intelligentization, and mechanization" by 2027, and it is investing heavily in microelectronics, artificial intelligence, quantum computing, and hypersonic missiles. It is widely believed that a substantial part of this modernization drive is built on U.S. technology. As a senior Biden administration official said, "We believe certain advanced computing capabilities which rely on U.S. chips, software, tooling and technology are fueling [China's] military modernization...." For example, computers designing and testing China's hypersonic and other missiles run on U.S. software and semiconductors. A Washington Post investigation found over 300 sales of prohibited, U.S.-origin software to Chinese missile developers. Scientists involved in these programs described "almost unfettered access to U.S. technology."

Incredibly, a large number of the sales involved software that the DoD paid American companies to develop. Consequently, U.S. taxpayers are paying for products that China surreptitiously acquires and then integrates into its own military programs. Similarly, much of the Chinese capability to break U.S. military and diplomatic encryption depends on quantum computing using U.S. technology. Improvements in drone warfare and unmanned naval vessels also depend heavily on U.S. semiconductors and software, not just for their guidance systems, but also for targeting algorithms.

Every techno-military innovation that China acquires from the United States accelerates its military modernization and allows it to spend more on other military priorities. And despite public proclamations of spending only $220 billion on its military in 2022, China's military spending is quite large and rapidly growing. According to a U.S. intelligence estimate, in 2022 China really spent approximately $700 billon on its military. The wide discrepancy results from China omitting broad categories of military spending, and by calculating the spending at market exchange rates instead of at purchasing power parity rates, i.e., unadjusted for local costs, especially less expensive personnel costs.

Technology denial as dominant U.S. policy tool

The change in the military balance would be less concerning for the U.S. if China were not so determined to unify with Taiwan, the source of 90% of the world's most advanced semiconductors and a cornerstone of U.S. defense strategy in East Asia. General Secretary Xi now regularly discusses how unification with Taiwan will occur by 2027, even if this means war, and U.S. Secretary of State Anthony Blinken said China is "...determined to pursue reunification on a much faster timeline." Some senior U.S. military officials now speak of a dangerous "window," or the few years remaining between now and 2027, when China "will" attack Taiwan if it has not already unified with it.

Given the China war danger, the traditional response by many U.S. policymakers would be to increase both the size of the U.S. military and the amount of money spent on it. Now, however, such a response is difficult because of the enormous growth in U.S. federal debt. Since the 2008 Global Financial Crisis, the U.S. has run staggeringly large fiscal deficits, and as a result, total outstanding federal debt in January 2023 equaled $31.9 trillion or 119% of GDP. (See Figure 3.) Under such circumstances, it is difficult to see how the U.S. can significantly and sustainably increase defense spending barring the outbreak of a war with China. Given this inability to spend its way out of the China challenge, as well as a desire not to allow China to change the status quo in east Asia, the U.S. must look to other policy instruments to slow China's military advancement and deter it from using force to change the status of Taiwan. The most obvious instrument for reestablishing U.S. military primacy, and potentially reversing U.S.

Fig. 3: High Debt to GDP Ratio Poses Defense Spending Problems

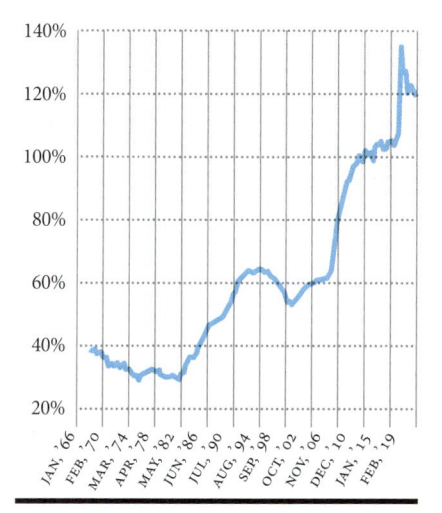

SOURCE: Federal Reserve Bank of St. Louis.

economic decline, is domestic and international economic policy.

Domestically, the Biden administration has already instituted far-reaching industrial policies designed to buttress America's domestic economic and technology strength. The most notable technology part of these policies is the CHIPS and Science Act, a $52.7 billion federal subsidies program to support semiconductor research, development, and manufacturing. Approximately three-quarters of the funds will be allocated over the next five years for the construction of semiconductor fabrication plants, or "fabs," in the U.S. Internationally, the administration is trying to take advantage of both the U.S.' still-competitive technology innovation position, and its dominance of the international financial system to throttle China's own diversion of technology resources into military activities. Concurrently, the administration also wants to engage China diplomatically while pivoting its defense policy toward one more fit for deterring a Chinese attack on Taiwan. Enhanced technology export controls and potential restraints on outbound investment to China are the central components of this strategy.

Export controls

The Biden administration significantly expanded Trump administration technology transfer restrictions by placing stricter limits on the sale to China of advanced technology such as 7-nanometer or smaller semiconductors. It also stopped advanced semiconductor sales without export licenses to any Chinese company, not just designated companies, and it prohibited U.S. citizens and permanent residents from working for, or with, Chinese semiconductor manufacturers or advanced software designers. This employment prohibition is expected to prove particularly vexing for Chinese companies, since a significant number of key research and development positions are held by Americans. The administration also finally won Japan and the Netherlands' agreement to restrict sales by their companies to China of semiconductor manufacturing equipment.

U.S. National Security Adviser Jake Sullivan described the administration's approach as a "small yard, high fence" that make it difficult for China to obtain a narrow range of technologies with military applications. However, as an indication of how contentious even these steps were, the Administration gave a one-year exemption to South Korean and Taiwanese companies producing prohibited semiconductors in China, and then extended those exemptions through October 2024. Regardless, the restrictions had an impact; Chinese customs data for the first 6 months of 2023 indicated a 22% decline in value terms of semiconductor imports. The controls did, and are, making it more difficult for China to obtain the necessary inputs for advanced manufacturing of both military and civilian products. However, the utility of the effort has been called into question, given China' ability to seemingly continue to technologically innovate.

In September 2023, during a visit by Commerce Secretary Gina Raimondo to Beijing, China's Huawei Technologies unveiled the Mate 60 Pro, a 5G phone utilizing a 7-nanometer chip. Huawei was first sanctioned in May 2019 by the Trump administration, and its primary Chinese semiconductor supplier, Semiconductor Manufacturing International Corp. (SMIC), was sanctioned in December 2020. It is unclear how SMIC produced the chips for Huawei, and the capabilities of the chips remain to be seen. Nonetheless, Huawei seems to have accomplished something that sanctions advocates thought it could not do.

One of the problems with semiconductor export controls is that the U.S. government has difficulty getting American and foreign companies to comply with the restrictions. *The Wall Street Journal* describes the relationship between the government and the technology companies as one of "cat-and-mouse," where the government announces restrictions and the companies circumvent them. Matthew Pottinger, then a deputy national-security adviser to President Trump, accused the Commerce Department, which is the department primarily responsible for export control enforcement, of being too aligned with business and not serious about stopping threatening technology transfers. Given that the Commerce Department traditionally granted virtually all export license requests, and given that current license application declinations have risen to 26%, this charge probably had merit.

One of the more egregious examples of export control avoidance was Nvidia's tweaking of the prohibited "A100" chip that is important for large data centers conducting artificial-intelligence calculations. Nvidia redesigned the chip to fall just below the prohibition threshold while essentially maintaining most of its performance characteristics. The U.S. government eventually outlawed the sale of even these chips, but not before China has an additional year to purchase the modified version. Nvidia defends its action, saying the export licensing process "…will make our sales and support efforts more cumbersome, less certain, and encourage customers in China to pursue alternatives to our products, including semiconductor suppliers based in China, Europe, and Israel." Given that more than a quarter of Nvidia's $26.9 billion in fiscal 2022 revenue came from China and Hong Kong, their position is not hard to understand.

Semiconductor companies are also

A Semiconductor Manufacturing International Corp. (SMIC) Kirin 9000s chip taken from a Huawei Technologies Mate 60 Pro smartphone in September 2023. The chip uses a 7-nanometer processor and it may indicate that China is making progress in its push to circumvent U.S. export controls and build its own advanced domestic semiconductor sector. JAMES PARK/BLOOMBERG/ GETTY IMAGES

able to minimize the impact of the export controls by weakening the regulations before they are adopted. As the Biden administration and some Congress members moved to strengthen export restrictions, companies and their trade associations and lobbyists quietly and effectively moved to neuter the restrictions. The Chamber of Commerce and the U.S.-China Business Council are particularly active in opposing increased semiconductor restrictions. As an example, when SMIC was added to the Entity List in December 2020, the restrictions on semiconductor manufacturing equipment were written to include only those technologies "uniquely" capable of producing semiconductors at 10-nanometers in size or smaller. Since most semiconductor manufacturing tools can manufacture chips of different nanometer, the regulation barred a very small number of machines. This very large loophole was obvious when the regulation was promulgated, and in 2022 Chinese companies still imported $14.5 billion of advanced semiconductor manufacturing equipment from U.S.-based companies.

Besides weakening the rule and then gaming them when they are promulgated, companies also push for extended deadlines before the regulations take effect. This happened with ASML, a Dutch firm with a near monopoly on advanced chip making equipment. While the Dutch and U.S. governments agreed to impose tighter restrictions on chip manufacturing equipment in January 2023, the final date for shipment was extended to January 1, 2024. As a result, Chinese imports of Dutch-made lithography machines (mainly form ASML), increased 64.8% during the first nine months of 2023. Given the porousness of the export controls, one might ask why it took Huawei and SMIC so long to produce a 7-nanometer chip.

Outbound investment controls

The second part of the denial strategy concerns restrictions on U.S. (and ultimately allied) companies seeking to invest in China's technology sector. Limiting outbound investment to China is not primarily about limiting capital flows. At least thus far, the world is still awash in capital and there are many countries, such as Saudi Arabia, that are wealthy and eager to provide capital to China. The larger issue is the capital flows' positive spillover impact.

While there are issues around measurement and what parts of a local economy benefit most, the economic literature on the subject considers FDI's impact to be extremely positive, since it diffuses technical knowledge and better work practices. FDI enhances productivity growth, especially when research and development-intensive developed countries invest in

Employees assemble an ASML Twinscan XT1000 lithography machine at the ASML Holding NV factory in Veldhoven, Netherlands, on June 5, 2014. ASML is Europe's largest semiconductor-equipment suppliers. JASPER JUINEN/BLOOMBERG/ GETTY IMAGES

emerging economies, and this has a significantly positive effect on economic growth. Venture capital-financed start-ups, in particular, help commercialize new technologies while also promoting innovation. According to PitchBook, since 2016 U.S. venture investors participated in more than 700 Chinese artificial intelligence and semiconductor technology startups.

One of the more controversial venture capital funding experiences concerns Sequoia Capital, at the time an approximately $100 billion fund. In a 2019 interview with Chinese media, Neil Shen, managing partner of Sequoia Capital China, bragged about Sequoia's proprietary database, collected over 40 years, that held due diligence and other competitive information on all companies it had invested in. He referred to it as Sequoia's "most important competitive power." This is an example of the importance of intangible assets like patents and access to other experts that venture capital firms bring to China and how they foster positive spillover.

Neil Shen, managing partner of Sequoia Capital China, speaks during the Bloomberg New Economy Forum in Singapore, on Wednesday, Nov. 16, 2022. BRYAN VAN DER BEEK/BLOOMBERG/GETTY IMAGES

Sequoia was reported to have invested in over a thousand Chinese companies, including many in the technology sector. In at least one case, it invested in an artificial intelligence contractor for the PLA. Given the problem of dual use technology and MCF, it was likely that Sequoia "seeded" or otherwise invested in numerous technology companies that were a potential threat to U.S. security. After coming under intense scrutiny by the U.S. government, the firm decided to split into several companies, including a stand-alone China investment company domiciled and managed outside the United States.

The issue of access to capital, while not as critical as FDI positive spillover, may still be important because at the margin, it makes it easier for Chinese companies, including defense companies, to raise funds. For example, there is AVIC Xi'an Aircraft Industry Group (AVIC), China's leading aerospace firm. In the event of a U.S.-China military conflict, AVIC's products would kill Americans, and by virtue of its place in global and emerging market indexes and actively managed investment products, millions of American investors own AVIC. While the amount of AVIC in any individual American investor's portfolio may be de minimis, when one adds up the scores of Chinese companies involved in defense, cyber security, surveillance, and other potentially threatening areas, and multiplies this by scores of asset managers, the sums are meaningful. According to an analysis by Rhodium Group, U.S. investors held $1.1 trillion of Chinese equity and $100 billion in Chinese bonds at the end of 2020. If even 5% of this sum is security-related, it equals $55 billion. According to Rep. Gallagher, BlackRock alone, America's largest asset manager, has invested more than $429 million in more than 60 Chinese companies that "endanger U.S. national security or human-rights."

Both the Biden administration and Congress are active in proposing outbound investment restrictions, but the contentiousness of the issue is illustrated by how difficult it has been for either to produce any restrictions. The idea of outbound investment restrictions was first broached by the Trump Administration in 2018, when the administration realized that even after strengthening export and in-bound U.S. investment controls, Chinese companies could still evade them by having U.S. companies open factories in China and build the restricted technology there, or by having U.S. venture capital firms find and grow the most promising military or dual-use technology start-ups in China.

The Biden administration first publicly raised the outbound investment issue in July 2021, but the administration then spent two years deliberating over what type of restrictions are appropriate. Finally, in August 2023, President Biden signed an Executive Order (E.O.) requiring only that U.S. persons notify Treasury of "…transactions involving certain technologies and products that may contribute to the threat to the national security of the United States." It identified three categories of technologies and products to be covered: semiconductors and microelectronics; quantum information technologies; and artificial intelligence. The E.O. ordered the Treasury Department to continue reviewing the issue and produce a final rule by sometime in late 2024. Considering what many asked for, the Biden E.O. was modest. It excludes biotechnology and critical minerals. It targets provision of funds through mergers, private equity, and joint ventures, but portfolio (i.e., non-direct) investments seem excluded. It only restricts AI investments in explicitly military applications, and even in the three restricted sectors, investments are allowed if the Chinese firm earns less than 50% of its revenue from these restricted sectors. Additionally, no retroactive restrictions are considered, so any investment made before the future effective date would be "grandfathered in."

The American Enterprise Institute's (AEI's) Derek Scissors said the E.O. "…isn't "small yard, high fence." It's small yard and still thinking about how many holes in the fence." U.S. Senator Marco Rubio said the "…proposal is almost laughable. It is riddled with loopholes [and] explicitly ignores the dual-use nature of important technologies…" Rep. Gallagher criticized the E.O. for failing to address investment flowing into China's public securities markets, saying it leaves 85% of US investments in China unaffected. He added: "You don't defeat an adversary by shoveling millions of dollars into their military programs."

In 2023, the Senate passed an amendment to the National Defense Authorization Act that also considered

U.S. Commerce Secretary Gina Raimondo (C) hugs a young girl dressed in a LinaBell costume as she visits Shanghai Disneyland on August 30, 2023. ANDY WONG/AFP/GETTY IMAGES

outbound investment. It mirrored the administration's call for investment reporting and added three additional sectors of concern: hypersonics, satellite-based communications, and networked laser scanning systems with dual-use applications. AEI's Scissors wrote that the amendment "…brought more evidence of bipartisan consensus on China. Unfortunately, the consensus is do very little, while pretending otherwise…" Senator John Cornyn, the co-sponsor of the amendment, was frustrated by his inability to produce a tougher amendment and blamed "efforts by members, backed by industry that wish to continue to build the scale and technological capabilities of foreign adversaries."

The policy dilemma

As noted, the difficulty with the debate over technology denial is that U.S. policymakers cannot decide whether China is a national security threat or a business opportunity. If China is a national security threat, then all trade and investment can be detrimental to U.S. interests. It is difficult, and perhaps reckless, to promote economic integration with a country that is a military threat and a potential adversary in a war. Economic power is the foundation upon which military and political power rests, and when the United States helps China grow the economic foundations of its power, it further enables China's military and encourages its global political ambitions. A political realist approach would reduce economic interaction between the two countries to a minimum. Accordingly, when University of Chicago Professor John Mearsheimer looks at the U.S.' decades-long engagement with China, he sees what "…may have been the worst strategic blunder any country has made in recent history: there is no comparable example of a great power actively fostering the rise of a peer competitor."

If China is a business opportunity, then efforts to restrain technology trade and investment are a foolish self-denial of benefits. In the liberal trading world that the U.S. built, and into which it encouraged China to enter, the logic of the system largely encourages U.S. multinational corporations (MNC) to maximize profits regardless of a state's domestic political system, or – with limited exceptions – its foreign policy goals. Where profits come from is less important than their size and durability. As the investor and China critic Kyle Bass said: "If U.S. national security was left to corporate boardrooms, we would all be speaking Chinese tomorrow."

While U.S. business enthusiasm for trading with, and investing in, China has declined as China over the last few years pursued more punitive policies toward foreign corporations, the U.S. technology and financial service sectors are still the two sectors most interested in engaging with China. For the technology sector, existing and future profitability is deeply dependent on China. Besides Nvidia and ASML, other technology companies heavily dependent on China revenue include Broadcom, Intel, KLA, Lam Research, and Qualcomm. While Apple is partially a consumer product company, it also typifies the problem with the China technology relationship. Apple has become so dependent on China for iPhone production that rapidly moving out of China would wreck its profitability, and perhaps even its ability to compete globally. China never gave up on Huawei as its national handset (and telecommunications) champion, and if Huawei continues to undermine U.S. sanctions, Chinese pressure on Apple will increase. Similarly for Tesla, a self-described technology company. Its relationship with the Chinese government has become more troubled as China's own electric vehicle companies, especially BYD, have grown more successful. The tragedy for Elon Musk is that he almost single-handedly helped China rebuild its electric vehicle manufacturing sector after it floundered before 2017. This is a fantastic example of the positive spillover effects of foreign direct investment. And this spillover continues to have positive techno-military benefits for China.

Unlike the technology sector, the financial service sector's existing business model is less dependent on China. However, the possibility of huge future profits is hard to ignore. Accordingly, the financial service sector, especially asset managers, continue to strongly support U.S.-China economic integration. In 2020, the Wall Street Journal printed: "China Has One Powerful Friend Left in the U.S.: Wall Street." It detailed how China's then vice-premier Liu He and other senior Chinese officials in 2018 met top American financial executives and promised their companies future benefits in order to encourage them to support less hostile U.S. policies toward China. It also pointed out how many of these promised benefits never materialized. Still, financial service sector support for less hostile China policies is strong. To Representative Gallagher, Wall Street puts on its "golden blindfolds and chase a yield that never comes." However, private sector resistance to the denial strategy may be about more than just pecuniary self-interest.

A case in point is JPMorgan and its CEO Jamie Dimon. JPMorgan is America's largest bank, and it has managed one of the more ambitious China expansion strategies. The bank controls a Chinese mutual fund company, owns Chinese futures and securities businesses, and is well-positioned to engage in Chinese investment banking should it pick up. A robust technology and investment denial strategy is a threat to these businesses. However, CEO Dimon is positioning the bank as if substantial U.S.-China decoupling will not occur, and he repeatedly stated that JPMorgan will remain in China during both "the good and bad times." Presumably, his faith in JPMorgan's ability to continue operating in China is based on a strong commitment to the American dominated liberal international order, buttressed by the bank's ability to influence U.S. policy.

The open trading and investment system the U.S. constructed after the Second World War is the foundation of global prosperity. Decoupling would have, as Secretary Yellen noted, "disastrous" consequences not just for the U.S. and China, but for much of the world. Yellen and other administration figures have gone out of their way to reassure China –and the American business elite—that the U.S. does not support decoupling, especially when a "...growing China that plays by the rules can be beneficial for the United States." Separation of the globe into trading blocs could, according to an IMF study, reduce global GDP by up to 7%, and this does not consider all financial and economic channels of the disruption. Given how poor long-term global growth prospects are, 7% would be an enormous shock that would feed directly through to corporate profits. Global financial executives like Dimon want to do everything possible to stabilize the current system.

The technology and financial service sectors have a legitimate and legal ability to shape U.S.-China policy through the legislative and regulatory process. As noted, the technology sector in particular has availed itself of this process to lessen restrictions on advanced technology exports to China. (As a group, the "Electronic Manufacturing and Equipment" industry has, since 2019, become the second highest lobbying spender in the U.S. after the pharmaceutical industry.) But the finance and technology industries also have another large advantage. The U.S. government, to a large extent, must rely on these industries to carry out a technology denial strategy. Corporate compliance is supported by the threat of criminal penalties, but given the enormity of the task, these sectors usually have the upper hand except in all but the most egregious violations. There is nothing illegal, or perhaps even untoward about this. As capitalist democracies evolved, monarchs and then legislative bodies crafted compromises, first with merchants and financiers, and later with business elites, to gain their support for increasing state power and fighting wars. This was a major factor promoting the development of democratic institutions in much of the western world. However, the relationship between the state and what came to be known as the private sectors has always been both fluid and contested.

While there is some debate in the international political economy literature, some, such as the late political scientist Robert Gilpin, argued that as long as multinational corporations served the interest of the globally dominant state, in this case since 1945 the United States, their existence and growth was tolerated, if not encouraged. But now that the United States' dominant role in the international system is threatened, MNCs have greater opportunity to undertake activities that can be seen as antagonistic to the dominant power, i.e., the United States. This leaves U.S. executives with a degree of freedom to shape U.S.-China policy which previously did not exist. Regardless, public pressure on the U.S. government and/or corporate leaders can help shape the future outcome of this policy debate.

Chinese Premier Li Qiang (R) shakes hands with U.S. Treasury Secretary Janet Yellen during a meeting at the Great Hall of the People in Beijing on July 7, 2023. MARK SCHIEFELBEIN/AFP/ GETTY IMAGES

SINO-AMERICAN RIVALRY

Discussion questions

1. Is China a national security threat or a business opportunity? Can it be both?

2. If China is a national security threat, should a U.S. denial strategy attempt to slow China's overall economic development, or just its military development?

3. If China is a national security threat and a technology denial strategy is appropriate, how can the U.S. government obtain better compliance from its business sector?

4. Should U.S. investors, and their asset managers, be prohibited from buying and owning Chinese defense companies?

5. If China is a business opportunity, are there no products that should be sold to China? Where should the line be drawn?

6. Is the United States in a new cold war with China? Is it in a technology cold war?

Suggested readings

Allison, Graham, "The Thucydides Trap: Are the U.S. and China Headed for War?" **The Atlantic,** September 24, 2015. A discussion of the historical experience of power transition between empires, and then states.

Clay, Ian, and Atkinson, Robert D., "Wake Up, America: China Is Overtaking the United States in Innovation Capacity." (Information Technology & Innovation Foundation, January 23, 2023. Available at www.itif.org.) A comprehensive examination of predatory Chinese practices in the technology sector.

Doshi, Rush, **The Long Game: China's Grand Strategy to Displace American Order.** (Oxford, UK: Oxford University Press 2021.) An examination of China's long-term goals for displacing the United States as the globally dominant power.

Ikenberry, John G., Nathan, Andrew J., Thornton, Susan, Zhe, Sun Zhe, and Mearsheimer, John J., "A Rival of America's Making?" **Foreign Affairs,** March/April 2022. A debate of the culpability, if any, for promoting the rise of the U.S.' greatest competitor.

Miller, Chris, **Chip War: The Fight for the World's Most Critical Technology.** (New York: Scribner, 2022.) A deep dive into the importance of semiconductors in contemporary life and their role in the geopolitical competition.

Pottinger, Mathew, "Beijing's American Hustle: How Chinese Grand Strategy Exploits U.S. Power." **Foreign Affairs,** Sep./Oct., 2021. An examination of how China undermines the U.S.' power position.

Don't forget to vote!
Download a copy of the ballot questions from the Resources page at www.fpa.org/great_decisions

---

To access web links to these readings, as well as links to additional, shorter readings and suggested web sites,
GO TO **www.fpa.org/great_decisions**
and click on the topic under Resources, on the right-hand side of the page.

Nato's future
by Sarwar Kashmeri

Warships from various NATO member states taking part in the major maritime maneuver "Northern Coasts 23" in the Baltic Sea off the coast of Latvia in September 2023. The naval maneuver, under German leadership, practiced tactical procedures for national and alliance defense in near-coastal waters. The exercise, which was also aimed at strengthening cooperation between NATO countries in the Baltic Sea region, involved 3,200 servicemen and women from 14 nations. BERND VON JUTRCZENKA/PICTURE ALLIANCE/GETTY IMAGES

For anyone who believed that the North Atlantic Treaty Organization (NATO) had morphed into a grand old club rather than an organized military alliance of European and North American countries, the Russia-Ukraine war has been a pleasant surprise. Within days of the 2022 Russian invasion of Ukraine, the 29 (now 31) NATO countries had set up supply lines to funnel war-material into Ukraine, built plans to equip and train Ukraine's military, and begun to deploy NATO army, air-force, and naval resources to the Baltic countries adjacent to Russia. The quick mobilization was a muscular reminder to Russia that, should it invade a Baltic country, the Alliance was ready, willing, and able to invoke Article 5 of the NATO treaty—that requires every member of NATO to treat an attack on any one member as an attack on all, obligating the Alliance's members to help the attacked nation in every way possible, including with military force. To its credit, the Alliance had long ago created a military command structure equipped with the same NATO grade arms and ammunition. The Alliance's structure respects NATO member countries' independence, while also allowing their military resources to flow into NATO formations with interchangeable arms and ammunition to assemble a potent NATO fighting force. It is a structure that includes a parallel political framework to

SARWAR KASHMERI *is founder and host of the well-known video channel, Polaris-Live.com "U.S. and China in the World." A Fellow of the Foreign Policy Association and author of 3 books including NATO 2.0: Reboot or Delete. He speaks frequently to business, education, and military audiences.* i

facilitate consensus between member countries as different as Croatia, Turkey, Italy, and the United States. That framework is a critically important NATO function, given that every action taken by NATO requires approval by every Alliance member. Before long, U.S.-led sanctions to throttle Russia's economy were hammered out, as was backing to provide political support for provision of funds and advanced military equipment to Ukraine from the Alliance countries members' own defense inventories. At the same time, a delicate balance was struck to ensure that assistance for Ukraine would not go too far, entangling NATO itself in a shooting war with Russia. To date, over 150 billion dollars of aid has been channeled through NATO to Ukraine ($73 billion from the U.S. alone); the swift response has put paid to Russia's plans to crush Ukraine quickly and without military intercession of the West.

It was a performance of which the founders of NATO and the Alliance's members can be justifiably proud.

But the Alliance's response has also unearthed deep-seated weaknesses that still bedevil NATO. Those weaknesses include the continuing inability of the European Union, the richest group of countries in the world, to defend themselves without U.S. leadership, even in a Europe-centered conflict against Russia, a comparatively weaker foe with a defense budget smaller than France and NATO's bureaucratic and ponderous process of fighting wars, a cause of serious problems in past conflicts.

These internal political conflicts prevent the European countries from pooling their defense outlays and command and control mechanisms together. If not attended to, the weakness will jeopardize NATO's future existence. One only needs to think back a few years to the U.S. presidency of Donald Trump, during which he plainly criticized the continuing reliance of Europeans on American taxpayers for their defense. That sentiment has only grown, as evidenced by the October 23, 2023, supplemental budget compromise that could only be passed after the budget was stripped of any funds to support Ukraine in its conflict against Russia. How might this play out if Mr. Trump is reelected President of the U.S. in 2024?

NATO is now 74 years old, and the U.S. is still, as it has always been, the glue that holds the Alliance together. The Alliance's age means that most people present at its founding are no longer alive. And the history of its founding, the trials and travails that had to be crossed to create NATO, the compromises that had to be made, and the results of NATO's actual performance in battle are rarely remembered. Vital dynamics of NATO's history have been largely forgotten, most notably the occasional but serious schisms between the United States (NATO's de facto leader) and its European members. For instance, when the European members of NATO wanted to fight alongside the U.S. in Afghanistan after 9/11, the United States turned down their offer—a clear message to the Europeans that the United States believed that the state of their armed forces and their process of waging war by committee would hurt, rather than help, the fast-moving, hard-hitting American fighting machine.

One of the aims of this essay, therefore, is to reach out to the Great Decisions community to explain where NATO has come from, to forecast how NATO can continue to grow, and to provide examples from NATO's military engagements, with the hope of triggering a national discussion that generates ideas to strengthen and maintain NATO's future role in transatlantic security.

NATO—the history

NATO was one of several global institutions set up through the far-sighted American and European leadership after the Second World War to ensure peace, security, and growing prosperity throughout the world. These institutions include the United Nations; the World Trade Organization (or GATT—the General Agreement on Tariffs and Trade, as it was then called); the World Bank; the International Monetary Fund; and NATO.

As crucial as the other institutions were to the unprecedented wave of prosperity that would soon sweep the Western world, it was NATO that ensured the "free world's" steady march out of the chaos and destruction generated by the Second World War. It provided the security umbrella, confidence, and stability that the war-weakened European nations needed to rebuild themselves and heal the economic wounds of the Second World War.

To be sure, while the Soviet Union was a significant part of the Western alliance that destroyed the Nazi war machine, after the Second World War ended, the Soviet Union increasingly distanced itself from the alliance with Britain, France, and the United States while forcibly incorporating its neighbors into a new Communist empire. Within a year of the European war's end in May 1945, Russia's Communist leaders had gobbled up its Eastern, Central European, and Baltic neighbors. The Communist empire had now reached the boundaries of Western Europe. As Sir Winston Churchill, Britain's war-time Prime Minister, so eloquently put it,

"From Stettin in the Baltic to Trieste in the Adriatic an iron curtain has descended across the Continent. Behind that line lie all the capitals of the ancient states of Central and Eastern Europe. Warsaw, Berlin, Prague, Vienna, Budapest, Belgrade, Bucharest and Sofia; all these famous cities and the populations around them lie in what I must call the Soviet sphere, and all are subject, in one form or another, not only to Soviet influence but to a very

!Before you read, download the companion **Glossary** that includes definitions, a guide to acronyms and abbreviations used in the article, and other material. Go to **www.fpa.org/great_decisions** and select a topic in the Resources section. (Top right)

NATO'S FUTURE

North Atlantic Treaty Organization 1949 – 2023

NATO Enlargement

1949
BELGIUM
CANADA
DENMARK
FRANCE
ICELAND
ITALY
LUXEMBOURG
NETHERLANDS
NORWAY
PORTUGAL
UNITED KINGDOM
UNITED STATES

1952
GREECE
TURKEY

1952
(WEST) GERMANY

1982
SPAIN

1990
FORMER EAST GERMANY

1999
CZECH REP.
HUNGARY
POLAND

2004
BULGARIA ESTONIA
LATVIA
LITHUANIA
ROMANIA
SLOVAKIA
SLOVENIA

2009
ALBANIA
CROATIA

2017
MONTENEGRO

2020
NORTH MACEDONIA

2023
FINLAND

LUCIDITY INFORMATION DESIGN, LLC

high and in some cases increasing measure of control from Moscow."

The Soviets now stood eye to eye with the Western Europeans. It was commonly assumed that, sooner rather than later, the Communist march westward would continue. Using coercion, intimidation, and outright force, the Soviets would march into the Western European countries and add them to their burgeoning empire. Given the impoverished and weakened condition of Western Europe, there was little that these proud nations could do to defend themselves. They knew their real defense against Soviet domination lay across the Atlantic. Somehow, America had to become the guarantor of Europe's security.

With this aim in mind, Britain, France, and the three Benelux countries—Belgium, Luxembourg, and the Netherlands—signed the Brussels treaty in March 1948, a defensive alliance to demonstrate to the Americans that Europe was serious about defending itself against a Communist onslaught. The weakened state of the countries that signed the treaty, however, meant the pact would be powerless to fight a Soviet invasion of Western Europe without American might. In the autumn of 1948, the five members of the Brussels treaty invited the United States and Canada to formally join them in creating a transatlantic security pact.

The Brussels treaty was the genesis of the North Atlantic Treaty Organization. NATO came into being on April 4, 1949, in Washington, with the signing of the North Atlantic Treaty by 12 countries. Norway, Denmark, Iceland, Italy, and Portugal joined Britain, France, the Benelux countries, Canada, and the United States in the ceremony to create NATO. (The treaty is a model of brevity and clarity and is reproduced in its entirety at the end of this essay.)

Four important points frame the Alliance's birth, all of which have had an impact on its trajectory over the years. They are key to understanding NATO's present strengths and weaknesses:

NATO was the first external defense commitment made by the United States, ever. In his farewell address, President George Washington had warned the nation to avoid permanent alliances with foreign nations and to rely instead on temporary alliances for emergencies. That advice was scrupulously followed by the United States in the two world wars of the 20th century: The United States entered the First World War as an "associated" power, not an "ally" of Britain and France. This isolationist tradition continued through the Second World War. At the war's end, the Truman Administration made it clear that no foreign entanglements had been made among any of the allies. The NATO alliance broke this 173-year-old tradition.

The second point worth noting, as a cursory glance at the Treaty will show, is the close connection established by the signatories of the North American Treaty between NATO and the United Nations. This fact is either not generally known or conveniently overlooked these days.

The first line of the Treaty begins: "The Parties to this Treaty reaffirm their faith in the purposes and principles of the Charter of the United Nations…." Article 1 then states: "The Parties undertake, as set forth in the

51

Charter of the United Nations, to settle any international dispute in which they may be involved by peaceful means in such a manner that international peace and security and justice are not endangered...." Article 7 acknowledges the "...primary responsibility of the [United Nation's] Security Council for the maintenance of international peace and security."

The connection with the United Nations contextualizes European NATO members' refusal to let the Alliance join America's 2003 invasion of Iraq: Without the UN Security Council's approval, the American invasion of Iraq was deemed illegal.

The reverse was true with Afghanistan. The European members of NATO agreed to send troops from their countries to Afghanistan under a NATO flag because the United Nations specifically authorized the creation of ISAF—the International Security and Assistance Force. The United Nations mandate provided the Europeans the legal authority required for European troops to be in Afghanistan.

Third, it is interesting to note that Portugal, one of the founding members of NATO, was then a military dictatorship. This has been a conveniently-forgotten fact, given that discussions about letting Russia join NATO have been cut short with the argument that this would change the nature of the alliance. NATO, after all, is an alliance of democratic countries. Clearly, the founders of NATO had no such qualms, as an effective defense of Europe would require air-deployment from the United States that, given the times' technical limitations, would require refueling in the Azores, in Portugal.

And fourth, NATO is financed through two budgets. The first pays for the Alliance's common charges such as its Brussels headquarters, the staff to run its day-to-day operations coordination functions, and a small fleet of five AWACS aircraft and five drones. This budget is shared by each NATO member based on the country's Gross Domestic Product and is rarely the focus of dissent within the Alliance.

The second budget pays for deploying a NATO mission. Crucially, NATO does not have a standing military force. Once NATO has made the decision to deploy military forces, each member country decides how many resources it wants to contribute and pays for the expenses of its military deployment. The difference between the common charges and military deployment costs can be significant. During the height of the Afghanistan war, for instance, the United States' common funds payment for FY2009 was $721 million, while America's share for its military operations in Afghanistan (America had around 68,000 troops in Afghanistan during 2009), were $3.6 billion per month.

Even though NATO members have agreed to spending at least 2% of their GDP annually on defense, only seven of them fulfilled this commitment in 2022. This dereliction of the 2% rule is the basis for the continuing criticism by the U.S. that America pays more than its share for European defense.

Leadership of the Alliance was divided into two positions: a military head, the Supreme Allied Commander in Europe, SACEUR; and a civilian head of NATO's bureaucracy, politics management, and day to day operations, the Secretary General. American General Dwight Eisenhower was appointed NATO's first SACEUR and Lord Ismay from Britain the first Secretary General. By tradition, and in recognition of America's position as NATO's most powerful country by far, every SACEUR since Eisenhower has been an American, while the Secretary General has been a European. U.S. General Christopher Cavoli and Norwegian politician Jens Stoltenberg fill these positions as this essay is written.

With the formal establishment of NATO in 1949, the United States and its Western European allies ensured that any attempt at invading Europe by its then arch-enemy, the Soviet Union, would be met with Alliance's formidable military forces. Also, recognizing that America had a habit of disappearing after wars were won, NATO would ensure the continuing presence of the United States in Europe. In addition, 20th century European wars had historically one common denominator—Germany. NATO would enfold Germany in the alliance's embrace, ensuring that the country's power could be harnessed for the West's common good, as opposed to being the trigger for repeated European wars.

General view taken April 4, 1949, in Washington, DC, of the official signing ceremony creating the North Atlantic Treaty Organization (NATO). AFP/GETTY IMAGES

NATO'S FUTURE

NATO's founding history was superbly summed up by its first Secretary General. Asked by a reporter to explain NATO's purpose, Lord Ismay famously replied, "NATO was created to keep the Russians out, the Americans in, and the Germans down!"

The creation of a cohesive NATO of 12 (mostly) like-minded countries had been relatively smooth sailing so far. This was about to dramatically change.

NATO expansion, from 12 to 31

Fueled by the Soviet threat and lubricated with American dollars, NATO continued to expand. Greece and Turkey joined NATO in 1951. Germany finally joined NATO in 1955. (The Soviet Union and its allies countered German entry with the formation of the 8-nation Warsaw Pact—it would remain NATO's arch-enemy until the dissolution of the Soviet empire in 1989.) Spain became NATO's 16th member in 1982.

At this stage in its lifecycle, NATO was still a Western European alliance with a laser-like focus on one objective: To stop a Soviet invasion of Europe.

Then, in 1989, the unexpected happened. The Soviet Union simply collapsed. The West went to sleep one night under the ever-present threat of nuclear annihilation by the Soviets. The next morning, the Soviet Union was no more. NATO's awesome deterrent power had kept Europe safe for forty-two years. The alliance's security umbrella enabled the West to defeat the Soviet empire without firing a shot.

During the Cold War years, protected by NATO, Europe rebuilt itself from the devastation of the Second World War and emerged in a shiny new form—the European Union, a breathtaking integration of Europe's many nations into an intimate economic and political grouping, a process that still continues.

Should NATO have been disbanded when the Soviet Union collapsed, given that the alliance had met all its founding objectives? Opinions on this question were and are mixed.

As General Brent Scowcroft, then

The Czechoslovakian and Eastern German infantries performing training manuevers in the region of Bohemia, Czechoslovakia, on September 26, 1966. KEYSTONE-FRANCE/GETTY IMAGES

National Security Adviser and an architect of the policies that had brought about the cataclysmic changes in Europe, has put it: "I'm sorry that because we were fixed on near-term goals that we didn't think hard enough about how NATO had to change going forward. We focused on a 'Europe whole and free,' but what did that mean? What did it mean to NATO to have the reason for the alliance, [the Soviet Union and its Warsaw Pact] … disappear? We never faced up to that."

But in this rush to absorb the newly free nations of Central and Eastern Europe, NATO and the West sowed the seeds of future tension with Russia. Scowcroft, who once taught Russian history at the United States Military Academy at West Point, had never been entirely comfortable with NATO's expansion to Russia's doorsteps. He remembers, as he told me in a series of conversations for my book on NATO, being surprised at Russians acquiescing to NATO's expansion. "They com-

President Ronald Reagan chairs a session of his Commission on Strategic Forces, in the White House Cabinet Room in Washington, DC, on April 12, 1983. From left are: James Schlesinger, former Secretary of State Alexander M. Haig Jr., President Reagan, and Brent Scowcroft, National Security adviser to President Ford and chairman of the panel. CHARLES TASNADI/AP IMAGES

NATO Timeline:

1949: The North Atlantic Treaty Organization is founded to deter Soviet expansion and a revival of European militarism. The 12 original members are the United States, Canada, Britain, Belgium, Denmark, France, Iceland, Italy, Luxembourg, the Netherlands, Norway and Portugal.

1952: Greece and Turkey join in the alliance's first expansion.

1955: West Germany joins NATO. In response, the Soviet Union and seven countries in Eastern Europe form the eight-nation Warsaw Pact.

1982: Spain becomes the 16th member of NATO.

1991: The Soviet Union collapses and the Warsaw Pact is dissolved.

1999: Three former Warsaw Pact nations — the Czech Republic, Hungary and Poland — join NATO.

2001: Article 5 in the NATO treaty, which stipulates that an attack on any NATO member is an attack on all, is triggered for the first time after the 9/11 attacks on the United States.

2002: The NATO-Russia Council is formed to help NATO members and Russia to work together on security issues.

2003: NATO takes command of the International Security Assistance Force in Afghanistan (ISAF).

2004: The biggest NATO expansion to date as seven countries become members: Bulgaria, Romania, Slovakia, Slovenia, Estonia, Latvia and Lithuania. (The latter three are the only former Soviet republics to have joined the alliance.)

2008: NATO countries welcome Ukraine and Georgia's aspirations to join the alliance, angering Russia. In August, Russia wins a short war with Georgia [A war started by Georgia] over the breakaway regions of South Ossetia and Abkhazia, which Moscow recognizes as independent states.

2009: Croatia and Albania become NATO members.

2011: NATO enforces a no-fly zone over Libya [and help overthrow Libya's President Mummar Qaddafi.]

2014: NATO suspends most cooperation with Russia after its annexation of Crimea.

2015: NATO ends the ISAF mission in Afghanistan. The alliance remains in Afghanistan to train local security forces until the Taliban takeover in 2021.

2017: Montenegro joins NATO.

2020: North Macedonia becomes NATO's 30th member.

2022: Sweden and Finland explore the possibility of NATO membership after Russia's invasion of Ukraine. (NATO assumes lead role in arming Ukraine to defend itself against Russia.)

2023: NATO admits Finland; Sweden pending.

SOURCE: Associated Press

U.S. Secretary of Defense Robert Gates speaks during a seminar on NATO's New Strategic Concept held at the National Defense University at Fort McNair, in Washington, DC, February 23, 2010. Anders Fogh Rasmussen, Secretary General of NATO, also addressed the conference on the organization's future strategy. SAUL LOEB/AFP/GETTY IMAGES

plained, but they acquiesced," he told me, "And I think I underestimated what it was really doing to Russian attitudes. I think we all did. We were humiliating Russia, not intentionally, but nevertheless that was the net result." Likewise, Scowcroft questions whether NATO really benefited from the expanded membership. "We should have asked ourselves, what are we trying to do?… For example, what does Albania bring to NATO? You can say well, it helps us democratize Albania, but is that the job of NATO?"

The disintegration of the Soviet Union left the Central and Eastern European members of the now-defunct Warsaw pact floating in a no-man's land between Western Europe and Russia—the shrunken successor to the Soviet Union. These erstwhile satellite states, having just emerged from decades of dictatorial rule, had one overriding strategic objective—to institutionalize and defend their new-found freedoms.

To institutionalize their rebirth, these countries looked to membership in the European Union. For their defense, however, they wanted to join NATO. More than anything else, these countries wanted the iron-clad guarantee that Article 5 of the NATO treaty—an attack on one NATO member will be treated as an attack on all—would defend them. Who knew what a future Russia might look like? Better to get NATO insurance as quickly as possible.

NATO was soon swamped with membership inquiries from states that had just months before been part of the Soviet Union's Warsaw Pact, that had been created to battle NATO!

Would it have been better, for instance, to involve and try to integrate Russia into the evolving European security structure? And had that happened might the world not be faced with the Georgia–Russia war of 2008 and Russia–Ukraine war today? We'll never know, of course, but it could have happened. But it is worth thinking about as NATO thinks about transforming again into a global alliance by expanding to include countries in the Asia-Pacific region beginning with Japan.

NATO's evolution

Since its inception in 1949 NATO had seen itself, and had been seen, as a purely defensive organization. This singular mission expanded after the demise of the Soviet Union. NATO's mission then changed to proactively meeting threats from distant lands that

NATO'S FUTURE

could be thousands of miles from Europe. Defense Secretary Robert Gates, described this change during the NATO conference held in Washington, DC, February 23, 2010.

At the strategic level, the greatest evolution in NATO over the last two decades is the transition from a static, defensive force to an expeditionary force – from a defensive alliance to a security alliance. This change is a result of a new security environment in which threats are more likely to emanate from failed, failing, or fractured states than from aggressor states…and where weapons proliferation and new technologies make possible the specter of chaos and mass destruction in any of our capitals.

Between 1995 and 1999, the Alliance's mission would become more elastic and NATO's military power would, for the first time, be used proactively to stop a series of civil wars in Bosnia and later in Kosovo. So what was next? Indeed, what was this new NATO?

NATO now saw its future challenges as having been transformed from Soviet tanks rolling into Western Europe to far more complex and global threats, including proliferation of weapons of mass destruction and non-state sponsored terrorism. To meet these threats, NATO believed it had no choice but to go where the threats were, adopting an "out-of-area" strategy.

Out of area, or out of business, would henceforth be the guiding principle for NATO, and the out-of-area strategy was officially adopted on April 4, 1999, after a fair amount of dissent. Not everyone liked the idea of converting NATO into a world policeman.

NATO's structure

NATO is run from its political headquarters in Brussels, Belgium. Here NATO's senior political decision-making body, called the North Atlantic Council (NAC), oversees the military alliance through their appointed "CEO"—NATO's Secretary General.

NATO's forecourt sculpture, also known as the 'NATO Star,' is pictured at the new NATO headquarters in Brussels. EMMANUEL DUNAND/AFP/GETTY IMAGES

All member countries are represented on the NAC by a full-time ambassador-led delegation, a mini-embassy at NATO. Roughly 4,000 people work at NATO Headquarters on a full-time basis. Of these, some 2,000 are members of national delegations and supporting staff members of national military representatives to NATO.

The NATO Headquarters provides a site where representatives from both the civilian and military side of all the member states can come together in order to make political decisions on a consensus basis.

Meetings at NATO Headquarters take place throughout the year, creating a setting for dialogue amongst member nations. The key advantage to having permanent delegations at NATO Headquarters is the opportunity for informal and formal consultation on a continuous basis. Consultation between member states is a key part of the decision-making process at NATO, allowing Allies to exchange views and information prior to reaching agreement and taking action.

I have stressed the last two paragraphs because they are central to NATO's cardinal operating principle: decision by consensus. The key to understanding NATO is to remember that it functions under one inviolable rule: every decision must be unanimously agreed to by every member country. In fact, no votes are cast during its deliberations. Unanimity ensures that every member's voice carries equal weight. Ultimately, all 31 member-countries as diverse as the United States, Turkey, Germany, Bulgaria, Croatia, Latvia, and the rest of the 23 others must agree on every issue unanimously for the alliance to take any action. It is commendably democratic in principle, this decision by consensus, but has also regularly interfered in NATO's operations. NATO's deployment in Afghanistan, its last "hot war," will illustrate this weakness.

At regular intervals, when matters of great import are to be discussed, the North American Council's meetings are organized at the defense or foreign ministerial level. Even more important decisions call for a meeting at the level of heads of state or governments. At these high-powered meetings the ambassadors will take a back seat to their defense or foreign ministers, or even to their country's president or prime minister. The NAC, the alliance's top decision-making body, meets under the chairmanship of the Secretary General, who is appointed by the member countries to a four-year term.

55

NATO at war

NATO's way of fighting wars, and the weaknesses built into the Alliance's structure through "National Caveats," is best explained by its deployment in Afghanistan under the UN-authorized ISAF.

With its Afghan deployment, NATO had entered its new incarnation: As an alliance that will go anywhere in the world to fight and defend Euro-American peace and stability. At the height of the war, some 80,000 troops were deployed in Afghanistan: around 50,000 under U.S. command and some 30,000 that comprised ISAF.

The immediate problem faced by NATO was a mismatch in what the alliance's military leaders expected from NATO member nations and what these nations were prepared to deliver. Many NATO countries (and especially their populations) assumed the alliance was headed to a largely peaceful environment where their troops would help stabilize and rebuild Afghanistan. When they got there, they found themselves in the middle of a war that was assumed to have ended.

Waging a war in Afghanistan proved highly contentious for the Europeans. A German Marshall Fund poll conducted during 2009 showed that the preponderance of the NATO countries surveyed, with the exception of the United States, wanted their forces totally withdrawn. More than half of West Europeans and two thirds of East Europeans wanted to reduce or remove their soldiers from Afghanistan.

It is a breakdown in communications that mystified former United States NATO Ambassador, Nick Burns, who is now the U.S. Ambassador to the People's Republic of China. "I feel this very personally, because I was present at the creation of this policy in 2003, when NATO made the collective decision to go in," he told me. "We decided to go into a combat mission, it wasn't for a peacekeeping mission, and some of the allies [acted] as if this was a humanitarian mission."

Once it became obvious that the ISAF mission was in a sense premature—United Nations peace-keeping and stabilization forces go into a region after the fighting has stopped—there was an immediate problem for many NATO members who did not wish to involve their military in a fighting war, and had opted out of the fighting in writing. This meant NATO did not have an integrated fighting force on the ground. Having volunteered to go to Afghanistan and stake its reputation on the war, NATO was now faced with a conundrum of its own making—Part of the forces sent to Afghanistan could not be used on the battlefield. It should be noted that even with their country's National Caveats, the ISAF forces performed superbly, tragically suffering many casualties. The fact remains that there was no unified military command in Afghanistan. As one of America's leading defense experts and later U.S. Secretary of Defense told me during the Afghan war:

What's going on in Afghanistan right now is critically important for the future of NATO because we [the United States] and NATO have made it into a NATO project…. There is a significant difference of opinion among the 28 NATO members on that war. If that wasn't the

NATO Secretary General Jaap de Hoop Scheffer (L) talks during the informal working lunch of the NATO-Russia Council in Vilnius, on February 8, 2008. The NATO chief called on Afghanistan to improve its government and boost support for its security forces to step up the fight against the Taliban. Speaking at a NATO defence ministers meeting dominated by the conflict in Afghanistan, Secretary General Jaap de Hoop Scheffer warned that "governance must visibly improve." ETRAS MALUKAS/AFP/GETTY IMAGES

NATO'S FUTURE

case, then why do we have a situation where each nation has conditions on its troops being there?... Some of them are there just because they wanted to put a few people in there. They won't fight or take casualties, but they are there. I'm not second guessing their decision, I'm not saying that is right or wrong, but those are the facts. So, for us to skip around that and act like this is a unified NATO command is totally untrue. If it was a NATO effort, all those NATO troops in there would be fighting side by side, as the United Nations did in Korea. So this is really an untruthful fabrication. We have invented it.

This was a hugely important statement from one of America's most knowledgeable foreign policy and security experts, who has always been and continues to be one of NATO's strongest supporters.

Here's how the Congressional Research Service Report described NATO member countries' individual war-fighting rules and their impact on military effectiveness.

At the outset, NATO leaders faced considerable difficulty persuading some member states to contribute forces to ISAF…. Many allies committed forces to the NATO operation, then imposed restrictions—"national caveats"—on tasks these forces could undertake….[A]lmost half the forces in ISAF have some form of caveats…, restrictions that allied governments, or their parliaments place on the use of their forces…. [C]aveats pose difficult problems for commanders who seek maximum flexibility in utilizing troops under their command."

One can only imagine how General Eisenhower's landings on D-Day and the subsequent war on the European continent would have fared if he had to work under National Caveats to figure out what troops to send where to do what.

On an overnight visit to one of the U.S. Navy's aircraft carriers, I found myself seated at dinner between two senior naval officers whose ages differed by around 18 years. During dinner I asked the older officer what he thought about the North Atlantic Treaty Organization. His answer was an emphatic endorsement. "It is and will continue to be the most powerful alliance for safeguarding the world," he said. Later, during a conversation with the younger officer, I asked the same question. His answer was equally forthright but dramatically different from that of his comrade in arms. "I remain to be convinced that NATO serves a useful purpose anymore," he told me.

The answers from the two naval officers boiled the arguments down to their essentials. If two senior members of America's armed forces could have such divergent opinions about the greatest military alliance in history, does anyone really understand why, over 20 years after the end of the Cold War, NATO still exists and what its main purpose is?

The year 2025 will mark the 80th anniversary of the end of World War II. NATO dates to that period and is part of the burst of creative energy for global progress that found fruition in a number of institutions founded through U.S. and European leadership. The Alliance ensured Europe's peace and security, linking the historically separate nations of Europe in a unifying process that still continues. Europe has vastly changed over the 80 years. In terms of population, Gross Domestic Product (GDP), and world trade, the EU is the richest grouping of countries in the world. In spite of this progress, NATO, a predominantly European structure, continues to rely on the United States for its muscle. There is a danger in this construct; winds of change are beginning to blow through Washington, DC, that question American responsibility for Europe's defense. The winds have not yet reached gale force, and American and European leadership must ensure they do not by a serious examination of the structure and purpose of NATO. What would happen were NATO to be swept away?. Redesigned for the 21st century, could NATO still play an important role in the defense of Europe and for the transatlantic relationship?

President of Ukraine Volodymyr Zelenskyy (R) and NATO Secretary General Jens Stoltenberg meet the press following negotiations in Kyiv, Ukraine, September 28, 2023. KANIUKA RUSLAN/UKRINFORM/FUTURE PUBLISHING/GETTY IMAGES

NATO flag is seen a day after NATO Summit ends in Vilnius, Lithuania on July 13, 2023. Beata Zawrzel/NurPhoto/Getty Images

NATO'S FUTURE

Discussion questions

1. Did the U.S. need to get involved in defending Ukraine against Russia? Should the U.S. still be responsible for the defense of the European Union, especially given that the EU is the richest bloc of countries in the world?

2. Should the West have tried to include Russia in helping design a post-Cold War European security structure? Given recent developments (namely, Russia's invasion of Ukraine), should the West invite collaboration with Russia to develop a new security structure? If so, how?

3. One suggestion for the future of NATO is to put Europeans in all its top management positions, include SACEUR, and to turn over NATO operations to Europeans. The U.S. would be a member country, but not the Alliance's leader – does this seem feasible or attractive? What role should the U.S. play, if it were to cede its leadership role?

4. How should NATO's operations abroad—especially in regions beyond its borders—be seen by adversarial states, such as China

Suggested readings:

Bush, George H.W. and Snowcraft, Brent, **A World Transformed.** New York: Knopf, 1998.

Kagan, Robert. **Of Paradise and Power.** Vintage, 2007.

Kaplan, Lawrence S. **NATO 1948: The Birth of the Transatlantic Alliance.** Rowman & Littlefield Publishers, 2007. A richly documented study of the greatest transformation of U.S. diplomacy and the personalities that made it happen.

Kashmeri, Sarwar A. **NATO 2.0; Reboot or Delete.** Potomac Books, Inc., 2011. Provides extraordinary insights into NATO and the future of the transatlantic alliance.

Kashmeri, Sarwar A. **The North Atlantic Treaty Organization and the European Union's Common Security and Defense Policy: Intersecting Trajectories.** U.S. Army War College Press, 2011. https://press.armywarcollege.edu/monographs/572/

Kupchan, Charles A. "NATO's Hard Road Ahead." **Foreign Affairs.** June 29, 2022. The invasion of Ukraine has shown that NATO is back, but the reality is that it never went away. Despite its clean bill of health and demonstrable unity, NATO faces a thicket of thorny issues highlighted in this piece. (https://www.foreignaffairs.com/articles/ukraine/2022-06-29/natos-hard-road-ahead)

Don't forget to vote!
Download a copy of the ballot questions from the Resources page at www.fpa.org/great_decisions

---

To access web links to these readings, as well as links to additional, shorter readings and suggested web sites,
GO TO www.fpa.org/great_decisions
and click on the topic under Resources, on the right-hand side of the page.

Invisible Indonesia
by Charles Sullivan

Workers dry batik, a traditional Javanese textile, after dyeing process in coastal Pekalongan, Central Java, Indonesia, June 5, 2021. Pekalongan is a city known for batik, a traditional Indonesian method of using wax to resist water-based dyes to depict patterns and drawings, usually on fabric. This textile has traditionally been crafted by hand in family workshops and small-scale cottage industries.
GARRY LOTULUNG/NURPHOTO/GETTY IMAGES

Indonesia, despite being the world's fourth most populous nation, remains essentially invisible to most Americans. Historically, the two nations haven't had a particularly close relationship. The United States had a rather limited contact with Indonesia during the Dutch colonial period, and Indonesians themselves have not immigrated to the United States in large numbers relative to Filipino, Vietnamese, Laotian, Hmong, and Thai immigrants, whose homelands have been the subject of more-direct U.S. intervention.

The idea of the country only emerged toward the end of the Dutch colonial era in the early 20th century. Building a new national identity from a large population that is highly diverse ethnically, linguistically, and culturally, and spread out over a broad archipelago, has not been a simple task, and the

CHARLES (CHARLEY) SULLIVAN *first arrived in Indonesia at the age of 3, with his U.S. Foreign Service family. He majored in history at Princeton, doing independent work in Indonesian history. He continued his training in Southeast Asian history at the University of Michigan. After a two-decade break he returned to complete his PhD at Michigan in 2020. His dissertation, made possible with support both from a Fulbright Scholarship and from the American Institute for Indonesian Studies, examines the cultural tensions leading up the Indonesian killings of 1965–66.*

> 'America doesn't understand what Indonesia is doing. It's frustrating.'
>
> Luhut Binsar Penjaitan, Indonesian Coordinating Minister for Maritime Affairs and Investment, August 2023

resulting nation has a complex history representing the interplay of the rich and varied cultures that have become part of Indonesia's national identity. To understand Indonesia, and why it does what it does, therefore, requires outsiders to undertake deep study of the nation.

But while the study of Indonesia, and particularly of its national development across the 20th century, has a rich academic history among specialists within the United States, few Americans have anything beyond a simple understanding of the nation, and almost none of them can speak its language. Despite being one of the world's most widely spoken languages, Indonesian is barely taught in the United States. It is offered regularly in only 13 universities, and it is not taught at all at the K–12 level. Beyond that, Indonesia has a very limited place in the American curriculum, perhaps coming up around orangutans and the "Ring of Fire" for elementary students, who also may or may not connect the search for a global trade in spices, the "discovery" of America and the naming of Native Americans as "Indians" to the "Indies."

Yet for Indonesians, their own sense of their world and their identity is very much connected to the complex details of their own national experience. It is that gulf of knowledge that General Luhut Panjaitan addressed in his interview about international reactions to Indonesia's changes in its trade policies about their nickel reserves with Peter Goodman for The New York Times. When Panajaitan said that Americans simply don't "understand" Indonesia's actions, he meant that we don't generally have the context to rationalize Indonesian decisions in the international arena, precisely because they are often driven by internal assumptions embedded in ideas of Indonesian identity that Americans know little about. This renders Indonesia largely invisible in American eyes; this article, in response, hopes to make Indonesia a little more visible, and understandable, to Americans.

A history of Indonesia

Indonesia is a new nation. While Indonesians had a long history of resisting Dutch and other European colonial presences, a shared national identity as subjugated colonial citizens only emerged when the earliest stirrings of nationalist ideas began among the scions of Javanese royal families in the first decade of the 20th century. Colonial oppression became a unifying force for Bataks, Malays, Sundanese, Javanese, Balinese, and Pamonan Dutch subjects in the Indies. But it was not until the early 1920s that nationalist leaders began to imagine the place they lived as a unified space they called Indonesia, describing the nation with a national conception based on shared geography, culture and language: "*Satu Nusa, Satu Bangsa, Satu Bahasa*"—"One Archipelago, One People, One Language." Each of these elements is still important for understanding Indonesia today.

Satu Nusa

"One Archipelago" refers to the idea that the nation stretches from Aceh in Northern Sumatra to Irian Jaya (West Papua, New Guinea), aligned with the map of Dutch colonial possessions that had seen significant expansion in the 19th century. When the Dutch state replaced the Netherlands East India Company as the controlling colonial interest in 1800, the Dutch military, beginning with the Java or Dipanegara War (1825–30,) forcefully brought most of the archipelago under direct Dutch control and administration.

But in 1910, at the outset of the Indonesian nationalist movement, the map had only recently been consolidated to include both Aceh in Northern Sumatra and Southern Bali. As this newly expanded map of the Dutch East Indies hung both in colonial offices and schoolrooms, the image of one archipelago presented as a consolidated colonial polity gave shape to the nationalist conception that Indonesia was comprised of *Satu Nusa*.

Satu Bangsa

Along with the idea of a single archipelago came the concept of Indonesians being one "people," or *bangsa*. The word implies a common ethnic grouping, but was used here to represent a new, non-ethnically based identity shared by all "native" peoples of the archipelago. The Dutch resisted this burgeoning sense of Indonesian unity, largely by reinforcing the idea that natives of different areas each had their own *adat,* or "traditional law" and customs. Javanese or Batak or Sundanese "traditions," largely identified and defined by Dutch scholars, became the legal basis of the colonial power assigned to local nobility, who ruled, but were led in doing so by their Dutch "elder brother," the colonial administrator in any given region.

Despite Dutch efforts to "divide and

! Before you read, download the companion **Glossary** that includes definitions, a guide to acronyms and abbreviations used in the article, and other material. Go to **www.fpa.org/great_decisions** and select a topic in the Resources section. (Top right)

INVISIBLE INDONESIA

conquer," Indonesian colonial subjects began to develop a common identity at the beginning of the 20th century. Indonesia's first mass political movement, *Sarekat Islam,* (SI, or "Islamic Union"), began around 1910. "Islam" here did not initially refer to religion; rather, it meant "not Chinese," as the first organizations that came to be SI arose in Central Javanese batik production houses against the presence of larger-scale Chinese textile businesses.

SI grew from under 5,000 members in 1912 to over 300,000 only three years later, and moved its focus from the economic politics of the fabric trade to a general anti-colonial movement. As it progressed, SI moved its aims from beyond questions of economic access to focus on self-determination and the development of local democratic institutions.

SI grew to several million members by 1920, and began to reflect cultural and ideological splits already visible in local colonial society. The organization essentially divided into three groups: the *"Abangan"* (Red) group, a largely rural group that mixed local village cultures and "traditional" forms of Islam that were also later combined with Marxist ideas (Red refers to the soil, not to Marxism); the *"Santri"* (orthodox Islamic scholars) group, a more modernist Muslim group that was centered around towns and cities, often with connections to Islamic boarding schools and small business; and a *"Priyayi"* (royal and administrative elite) group with connections to higher levels of formal Dutch education and to the military power that had been invested in the royal courts. The *priyayi* also had strong connections to cities, even as their sources of funding came from appanage lands attached to the dynastic ruling families, and formed the core of "modern" Indonesia.

These three groups came to be called the *"aliran,"* or streams, of Indonesian society. While these streams intermingled, often quite significantly, this idea of three cultural groups, each centered in its own geographical, economic and cultural spaces, became an organizing idea for the political balance within the emerging Indonesian national identity.

Satu Bahasa

Finally, *Satu Bahasa,* or "One Language," reflected the decision by early nationalists to adopt a form of Malay as a national language, renaming it *Bahasa Indonesia,* or Indonesian Language. There were several advantages to this. First, Malay's historical function as a primary language of trade across the region ensured that the language was widely known by Indonesians of all backgrounds. Second, it was precisely *not* Javanese, the language of the culturally and politically dominant and largest ethnic group. Unlike the extremely hierarchical Javanese, Malay is a largely egalitarian language, reinforcing the idea that all Indonesians are "one people."

Indonesia's enduring national identity

The idea of Indonesia as *Satu Nusa, Satu Bangsa, Satu Bahasa* has proved incredibly durable. Indonesia's national identity is strongly shared across the country, and pride in its culturally diverse population is fully incorporated in the concept of national unity: *Bhinnekka Tunggal Ika,* essentially translating as "Unity in Diversity." This concept of unity was to be expressed practically through the values of the national state philosophy, *Pancasila,* ("Five Principals") developed by Sukarno in 1945—monotheism, humanism, national unity, consultative democracy, and social justice.

But this unity did not come without struggles, both against the Dutch and internally. The Indonesian nationalist movement strengthened across the 1920s and 1930s, but its leaders (including Sukarno, Mohammad Hatta, and Sutan Syahrir) were sent into internal exile as their influence grew. The Japanese invasion of Indonesia (1942–45) brought a quick end to Dutch colonial rule, and initially, the nationalists worked with the Japanese under the Greater East Asia Co-Prosperity Sphere. But Japanese policies that violently extracted labor and commodities from Indonesia largely pushed the nationalist movement away from formal support of the occupation.

Forced into action by youth activists by the Japanese surrender at the end of World War II on August 15, 1945, Sukarno and Hatta declared independence on August 17. Arguing that the Indonesian nationalists had collaborated with the Japanese, however, the Dutch returned with the intention of regaining control of their prize colony. The Indonesians then fought a bloody four-year revolution against the Dutch to make that independence a reality. Ultimately, the United Nations forced the Dutch withdrawal from the islands through the Round Table Conference in The Hague in November 1949.

Faced with actual independence and sovereignty, Indonesia then began the difficult process of governing. Sukarno, leader of the Indonesian Nationalist Party (*Partai Nasionalis Indonesia,* or PNI) that had been the primary political opposition to the Dutch, was appointed Indonesia's first president.

The Sukarno era, 1945–65/66

In the first years of independence, all was new, and there were not many established structures or practices in place. The government cycled through a number of cabinets, designed largely to afford the new, often shifting political parties space in the national leadership, but based also in the idea that the nation's elites, centered in cosmopolitan spaces, were the ones most qualified to make important decisions in running the new nation. The Indonesian Communist Party was not represented in them, however, and by design, the military was excluded from positions of political representation, and military personnel did not vote.

In 1955, the first national elections were held to choose members of Indonesia's bicameral parliament. While the elections were contested by 34 different parties, the four large winners were Sukarno's nationalists; *Masyumi,* a coalition of modernist Muslim organizations; *Nahdlatul Ulama,* representing traditionalist Muslim communities, largely in Java; and a surprise showing from the Indonesian Communist Party (*Partai Komunis Indonesia* or PKI.) That is, the three *aliran* all had some form of representation, and much of the political power in the new parliament lay outside the capital, Jakarta.

The lack of a clear mandate to any party threatened the nascent feelings of national unity. Particularly contentious had been efforts of certain Islamic groups to make Indonesia an Islamic nation. Some of these groups, most of them under the *Masyumi* umbrella, aligned themselves with regional military commanders in the "outer" islands of Sumatra and Sulawesi. Those regional commanders took control of local governments in late 1956, largely in protest of expanding Jakarta's control of the regional military structure, as well as the capital's inability to provide sufficient funding to the armed forces. The Masyumi elements also insisted that Communists be removed from positions of power and influence, reflecting significant ideological differences and long-held tensions between those two *aliran*.

Guided democracy

As a result of this increasing inability to unify the nation, Sukarno suggested that western-style party-based democracy was not aligned with Indonesian concepts of governance, and that Indonesia would benefit from rule by a strong, central government, that would, of course, be led by him. Between 1957 and 1960, with strong support from the central military elite in Jakarta, Sukarno increased his control of the state apparatus by replacing elected officials with appointed ones and nationalizing important elements of the economy. Responding to the regional military and Islamic "rebellions," Sukarno declared martial law in 1957, ceding effective control of most of the country to the centralized military. *Masyumi* was banned in 1960 for its support of the rebellions.

Sukarno rationalized his changes to the government in his Political Manifesto *(Manipol)* that he delivered as part of his 1959 National Day speech, in which he urged Indonesians to "Rediscover our Revolution." Beyond the structural elements of his manifesto that gave the presidency more power, Sukarno also focused on building an Indonesian "national identity" *(Kepribadian Nasional),* which raised up cultural elements that he felt would be common to and benefit all Indonesians.

To some extent, his exercises around creating national identity were an attempt to calm the cultural, economic, and political volatility that had marked Indonesia's early years and the widespread fears of "moral crisis" that accompanied it. Moral crisis became a catch-all phrase for all the ills that many Indonesians watching the explosion of new, modern metropolitan life in the quickly growing large cities feared would afflict the nation if Indonesian life were to become too "western," or if change were to happen "too fast" or to go "too far." Critics pointed to corruption among government officials, economic gouging by local traders, and the luxurious lifestyle of cosmopolitan elites as repercussions of cultural change.

Confrontation and the end of the Sukarno era

As he sought to consolidate his power, and to bring the various political groupings into some sort of control underneath his leadership, Sukarno expanded this idea of harnessing national culture to call Indonesians to "finish the Revolution." In doing so, he encouraged Indonesians to confront threats from "neo-colonial" enemies both external and internal. In this process, perfecting Indonesian identity served as a foil for the challenges that threatened to pull the nation apart.

Externally, Sukarno focused on the *Konfrontasi* campaign against Great Britain's plans in 1963 to establish Malaysian independence, which included incorporating the British colonies of Sabah and Sarawak in Borneo as part of the new Malaysia. While military action was quite limited in the small-scale border skirmishes that resulted, the call to "Crush Malaysia" became a major political campaign to harness Indonesian revolutionary ardor. In National Day speeches, Sukarno called on Indonesia to "Stand on its Own Feet" and, famously, to enter a "Year of Living Dangerously" in 1964.

All three of the *aliran* took up the revolutionary call, adopting Sukarno's policies and slogans, but each also adapted the cultural elements of *Konfrontasi* to match their own ideological outlooks. A serious power struggle ensued, bringing into conflict the military, supported by Islamic organizations,

President Sukarno, the first leader of Indonesia after it became a republic in 1945, inspects his troops. HULTON-DEUTSCH/GETTY IMAGES

and the Communist Party. Armed conflict seemed inevitable, with rumors of the creation of a peasant Fifth Column on the Communist side, armed with smuggled Chinese weapons, and of a possible council of senior military officers backed by the CIA, which intended to overthrow Sukarno.

Tensions erupted the night of September 30, 1965. In the middle of the night, men dressed in green uniforms were led by junior military officers to the homes of seven members of the military general staff. They kidnapped and killed six of the seven generals and the adjutant, a lieutenant, of the other. Members of Sukarno's palace guard took over *Taman Merdeka,* Jakarta's central square, the site that holds the palace, the national monument, the offices of the Indonesian national radio, and the U.S. Embassy. At 10:00 am, the commander of the palace guard, Lt. Col. Untung, gave a nation-wide speech on the radio announcing that the *Gerakan Tigapuluh September* ("Thirtieth of September Movement," or G-30-S), led by a group of officers "loyal to President Sukarno," had acted to protect the president from a coup being planned by a "Council of Generals."

The broadcast characterized the Council as a "subversive movement sponsored by the CIA." Lt. Col. Untung's address explicitly challenged the existing military hierarchy in Indonesia, which he charged as elitist, privileged, and out of touch with the nation's communal, socialist values. His declaration called on members of the military to "scrape away the influences of the Council of Generals and their henchmen in the military."

However, the September Thirtieth Movement was almost immediately subdued. None of the Movement's plans came to pass. By the evening of October 1, Major General Suharto, the commander of the Army Strategic Command, retook *Taman Merdeka* and reclaimed the radio station. He addressed the nation in a speech at 10 pm. In language nearly identical to Untung's earlier broadcast, Suharto positioned both himself and the Army as the protectors of the Indonesian Revolution. President Sukarno, Suharto claimed, was "safe and sound" under the army's care.

Less than 12 hours after the G-30-S troops took over *Taman Merdeka,*

Suharto was in control of the capital and the Movement in Jakarta had been quashed completely. Even so, the Movement's brief presence marked a critical shift in Indonesian history.

Suharto's New Order, 1966–89

Over the next six months, the military took complete control of the Indonesian nation. Blamed by Suharto for coordinating the kidnapping and killing of the generals, the Communist Party was banned, and the army killed—often brutally—up to a million Indonesians connected to the Communist movement as they answered Suharto's call to "eradicate the PKI down to the very roots." Others, particularly leaders of leftist organizations, artists, and authors, were sent into internal exile in some of the same camps the Dutch had used to imprison nationalist leaders. Sukarno was removed as president in March 1966, and Suharto took power as Indonesia's second president, fully supported by the military in what came to be called the New Order (*Orda Baru*) government.

Although Indonesia's military leadership had significant training from the U.S. government in the 1950s and 1960s, there is no strong evidence that the Americans or the CIA were behind the events of early October 1965, or that they were involved in Suharto's planning in the immediate aftermath of the events of the night of September 30. Indeed, new and important research by Australian historian Jess Melvin has established that Suharto sent messages to regional military commanders on the morning of October 1, ordering them to begin pre-planned actions against the PKI before the Communist authorship of the events had even been mentioned, much less established. Historian John Roosa's research demonstrates that Suharto almost certainly knew of the planned 30th September Movement before it carried out its plans to capture the generals.

So it is important to see that both the "coup" and the "counter coup" emerged from long-simmering domestic Indonesian tensions that had reached a fever pitch. But, that noted, it is important also to recognize that the United States and other western powers aligned themselves swiftly with Suharto, and quickly and fully supported Suharto's moves against the PKI. American support and aid, both financial and political, flew to the New Order government, and the United States would remain a key supporter of the Suharto regime for the next three decades.

Development, economic growth, corruption, and ethnicity

From an American perspective, Indonesia became the domino that didn't fall in the Cold War. From an Indonesian perspective, America became a friend whose support was critical as the New Order sought to reestablish a functional economy, albeit one where significant sectors remained under military control. Over the next 32 years, Indonesia opened its economy to Western investment, although often foreign actors paid significant sums to Suharto and his family (Suharto's wife, Bu Tien, was jokingly referred to as "Bu Ten Percent"), as well as to military commanders, ministers, and other high ranking government officials.

During the New Order, Indonesia's economy grew significantly. From 1965–98, Indonesia's GDP expanded at an average annual rate of over 5%. Investment in the oil and agricultural sectors increased strongly, and manufacturing grew from approximately 10% of the economy in 1966 to over 25% of GDP by 1997. Foreign assistance, which Sukarno rejected in the early 1960s (famously telling the United States to "go to hell with your aid"), was critical to enhancing national infrastructure, including the development of healthcare facilities down to the local level.

Large-scale private enterprise grew steadily. But the opportunity to develop these businesses was largely limited to the Chinese-Indonesian community. Permits to allow wealthy Chinese to develop large-scale economic enterprises—facilitated by large payments to Suharto and his cronies—were granted because the Chinese could not provide the basis for a political challenge to Suharto. Culturally, the Chinese were considered outsiders, not part of the *Bangsa Indonesia*. Nonetheless, Chinese conglomerates came to dominate the privately held elements of the new Indonesian economy (the military continued to control critical and profitable sectors as well).

Production of matte nickel at the PT Vale nickel plant, in Sorowako, South Sulawesi, Indonesia. Workers are seen supervising the flow of hot liquid metal as it flows from a furnace at the plant, which targeted a production of 75,000 metric tons in 2019. SOPA IMAGES LIMITED / ALAMY STOCK PHOTO

Legacies of 1965

The New Order's political focus was on unquestioned internal control. While political parties were allowed (excluding of course, the PKI) and regular elections were held, Suharto's political organization, *Golkar,* consistently emerged with unassailable majorities of the vote. *Golkar's* voting share grew from 62% in the 1977 legislative elections to 74% by 1997, increasing each electoral cycle. This didn't necessarily reflect the true level of support for *Golkar,* as Indonesia's elections during the New Order were *"sudah disukseskan,"* literally translated as "already successed"—or, in other words, fixed.

Golkar ran on two twin themes: First, that Suharto and the military were the inheritors of the Indonesian revolutionary legacy, and second, that the New Order government was the bearer of economic development for a culturally unified Indonesian nation. But both themes fostered policies that disempowered the swiftly growing Indonesian general population.

The campaign to establish the Suharto regime as the vanguard of Indonesian national identity facilitated policies that, in the analysis of political scientists and anthropologists, attempted to empty Indonesian society of any opposition to the regime. Perhaps most central to this policy was the development of what Indonesian historian Yosef Djakababa has called the *"Lubang Buaya Narrative."*

Lubang Buaya ("Crocodile Hole") is the site outside Jakarta where the kidnapped generals' bodies were dumped in a well, albeit one with no crocodiles. It quickly became a loadbearing narrative for *Golkar's* propaganda. Soon after the reversal of the September 30th Movement, the military created a false story of the gory, sexualized killing of the generals at the hands of members of *Gerwani,* the Communist-affiliated women's organization. This story was embellished over time, first through coverage in the media, then through an official military history of the Movement. The narrative was repeated annually on October 1, with national commemorations of the killings of the generals. A graphic 1984 dramatic film telling the official story of the coup was shown on national television on the first of every October. School children across the nation were taken to movie theaters to be shown the (nearly four hour) film in its entirety each year.

The New Order also specifically fostered a cultural policy that divorced Indonesian practices from any local cultural philosophies that could have become sources of criticism of the new government. In particular, the New Order instituted policies of strict control down to the village level, where all local leaders were required to be members of *Golkar* functionary groups, while their wives joined the New Order national organization *Dharma Wanita* and were required to monitor such things as compliance with family planning policies down to the household level. The goal was to depoliticize Indonesia's still significant rural population, which had been the base for the PKI, and to re-form them as a "floating mass," responding to the control of the omnipresent state.

New Order Indonesia in the international sphere

Officially, Suharto's foreign policy retained Indonesia's neutrality in the Cold War.

Regionally, Indonesia's foreign policy centered on creating conditions for strong international trade and on regional security within the Association of Southeast Asian Nations (ASEAN), which was established in 1967. Indonesia joined as a founding member along with other western-oriented nations Malaysia, Singapore, the Philippines and Thailand, all of whom either were or soon would be governed by autocratic, anti-democratic "strong men." Within ASEAN, Indonesia assumed a position of quiet leadership, often referred to as the "first among equals" of the membership. ASEAN's focus was largely (and remains today) to enhance Southeast Asian economic opportunity and to gently address regional issues without impeding on national internal politics. For Indonesia, it was also an opportunity to be seen as a "leading" nation in Asia, particularly as the Indonesian economy grew in scale and global presence.

Globally, Indonesia was generally a reliable vote for the United States at the UN, excluding votes surrounding Israel and Palestine, where it voted in line with the majority of the Global South. In 1973, Indonesia was rewarded with a position as a non-permanent member of the Security Council, a position it has held three times since. But Indonesian foreign policy across the New Order was largely quiet and compliant, deferring to the general trends of western bloc international diplomacy.

Indonesia's one foray into troubled waters involved the invasion of East Timor in early 1975, after a 1974 coup in Portugal led to the decolonization of its overseas holdings. The Indonesian occupation of East Timor, an expansion of the idea of the Indonesian nation stretching through "one archipelago," led to UN resolutions condemning Indonesia's presence there. However, Australia's recognition of Indonesian sovereignty over the eastern half of the island provided enough political cover to keep Indonesia in East Timor, which it called its "27th province," until October 1999.

Violence defined the Indonesian occupation of East Timor. The initial invasion lasted for four years, as local militias resisted the Indonesian military presence. The Indonesian army retaliated as they had against the PKI a decade earlier: with mass killings, rapes, forced relocation of civilians, and scorched-earth policies that led to widespread starvation. As a coup de grâce, when Indonesian troops finally left the new country of Timor L'Este, army-linked paramilitary groups destroyed much of the new nation's infrastructure on their way out.

Indonesian life in the 1980s and early 1990s was more prosperous—and more placid—than it had been previously. But this prosperity was predicated on obedience to the military-controlled government, with compliance enforced by constant low-level violence, intimidation, and fear punctuated by occasional outbursts by the military or their militias, particularly for any movement that appeared to threaten the regime's autocratic rule.

The economic lapse of 1998, however, led directly to the end of the New Order as Suharto stepped down from the presidency in response to large-scale student demonstrations, and then more generally supported riots in many of Indonesia's cities. Called the *Reformasi* (Reformation) of the Indonesian nation, a correction of first internal transition in 1965–66, this was as much about re-establishing Indonesian rights to democracy and self-determination as it was about the pressures of a suddenly failed economy.

"By early 1998," Australian historian Max Lane writes, "across all the student groups, the primary goal was to force Suharto from power and end dictatorship. The most radical wing of the students also wanted to make sure that the 'dual role of the military' ended; that the military got out of politics. Some others also were struggling for a full-blown participatory democracy and were calling for the formation of People's Councils wherever mobilizations were strong."

Following the shooting deaths of four student demonstrators by the National Police at Trisakti University on May 12, riots broke out for several days in many of Indonesia's major cities. The riots were aimed largely at Indonesia's Chinese population, the easiest symbols of both the economic difficulties and New Order political control, and they resulted in the deaths of nearly 1,200 ethnic Chinese, the rape of Chinese women, and the destruction of Chinese businesses. Unable to reassert control over the situation, Suharto stepped down from the presidency on May 21, replaced by his Vice President, B.J. Habibie. Technically, this was a continuation of the Suharto presidency, but for all intents and purposes, the New Order government had come to an end.

Reformasi and the return(?) of Indonesian democracy

While the New Order itself came to an end, New Order political and economic capitalist elites remained fully in control of Indonesia. Habibie's short presidency, (May 1998–October 1999) marked mostly by decisions to release political prisoners connected to the PKI, gave way to an equally short presidency (October 1999–July 2001) of Abdurrahman Wahid (called Gus Dur), the head of the traditionalist *Nahdhlatul Ulama,* who put together a so-called "National Unity Cabinet" reminiscent of the early days of the Republic, with the goal of bringing the nation together after the sudden changes of 1998.

Gus Dur took on several difficult challenges. Administratively, he abolished the Ministry of Information, which had served as the principal source of control of the media and the censorship of information in the New Order. He suggested to the Consultative Assembly that they lift legal prohibitions on Marxism, and in his personal capacity, he recognized the killings of Communists in 1965 as a national tragedy. Most importantly, he sought to remove the military from political power, the principal demand of the 1998 student movement.

But conflicts with both the military and members of the People's Consultative Assembly led to his impeachment in July 2001, the result of significant back-room pressure and manipulation by New Order powerbrokers. So, within three years of the student movement aimed at restoring democracy, the functional leadership of the New Order had managed to expel the first president who took them on and reassert their own control.

The pattern of back-room politics continued, despite Indonesia now functionally being an electoral democracy. Wahid was replaced by Megawati Sukarnoputri, Sukarno's eldest daughter, and Wahid's vice president, who served as president from 2001–04. The military continued to reassert much of its influence, and another former general,

Suharto announces his withdrawal from position as the president of Indonesia May 21, 1998. The economic crisis and politcal turmoil gave rise to frustration and anger, fueling outbursts of violence, along with a general sense of lawlessness and fear. Non-stop student demonstrations fighting for politcal reform led to repeated violent clashes. Tensions climaxed in May with wide spread rioting and finally, the ousting of the authoritarian president Suharto after 32 years of power. PAULA BRONSTEIN/GETTY IMAGES

Susilo Bambang Yudhoyono (called SBY, "Ess Bay Yay,"), was elected Indonesia's sixth president in Indonesia's first direct elections for president in October 2004.

Under SBY, Indonesia made significant moves to reduce poverty rates, which remained high in the aftermath of the Asian Financial Crisis. His basic policy was to provide basic assistance to Indonesia's poor, while expanding global access to Indonesian markets, for example, signing a free trade agreement with Japan in 2007. The rise of China's economy and its regional investment in Southeast Asia also served as an engine for Indonesian economic development. During SBY's ten years at the helm, Indonesia was able to rebuild its economy, but the political elites were simultaneously able to solidify their control of the system. Selection of candidates for office at all levels was increasingly not driven from the grass roots up, but rather was imposed by an increasingly dense web of interrelated dynastic party leaderships.

It was perhaps ironic then that SBY was followed in office by Joko Widodo, popularly called Jokowi, who rose to the presidency from being the mayor of Solo, one of the royal cities of Central Java. Jokowi did not come from dynastic power. Indeed, he was born in the slums of Solo, but entered business and made his own wealth as a furniture exporter. He became a highly popular mayor by personally assuring that city services for such things as picking up trash were carried out regularly and as planned, or that city office employees were at work carrying out their duties when they were supposed to be. He used this popularity to move on to be elected governor of Jakarta in 2012, where he carried out similar policies, and he was elected president in 2014.

Jokowi continued to work on good government efforts, but he found that the national-level bureaucracies and back-room politics made this quite difficult. Over time, his agenda has become quite responsive to the desires of powerful interests, and his formerly direct approach to the details of political service has receded.

Incumbent Indonesian president Joko Widodo gestures as he arrives for an election rally on the final day of campaigning in Jakarta on April 13, 2019. BAY ISMOYO/AFP/GETTY IMAGES

Widodo has made several moves in the foreign policy realm, but again, this effort has been fairly contained, particularly around issues of protecting fishing rights within Indonesia's borders from Chinese fleets in the South China Sea. Recently, he has used Indonesia's functional control of the world's nickel supply—nickel being critical to the manufacture of electric vehicle batteries, a massively expanding energy sector—to insist that secondary processing of the metal be carried out inside Indonesia, even if largely by (overseas, not domestic) Chinese conglomerates. His ban on exporting raw nickel ore has brought charges from the European Union through the World Trade Organization that they are unfairly being cut off from access to Indonesia's nickel supply because they are not invested in nickel processing in Indonesia. It was in response to this that Minister Luhut expressed his exasperation that Americans don't understand the Indonesian desire to control the wealth derived from their own commodities, or the long history and economic politics that make this an important intervention, and largely the first of its kind, by an Indonesian president.

In the end, the nickel issue is small potatoes, but understanding Indonesian history does point out its importance to Indonesians. And understanding Indonesian history also helps lead to an understanding of the increasing middle-class disappointment with President Widodo.

Unable to run for a third term, Jokowi has not officially thrown his support to any candidate, even the nominee of his own political party. But his son, who is too young to run for either the presidency or vice presidency, has become linked as the vice presidential candidate for one of the two major candidates, Prabowo Subianto.

The rise of Prabowo is the among the clearest indicators of the remaining power of the military-linked New Order. Prabowo, the ex-husband of Suharto's second daughter, is a former military man. Prabowo's first command was with the Special Forces in East Timor in 1976, and his troops played a strong role in the suppression of Timorese independence fighters. He was later, as a Lieutenant General, the commanding officer of the special forces which suppressed the student movement in Jakarta in 1998, and who were certainly responsible for the "detention" and torture of 23 student activists, only 10 of whom ever returned. In the aftermath of these events, Prabowo was discharged from the military and left Indonesia for a decade. But he returned in 2009 to serve as Vice Presidential running mate to Megawati, and ran, but lost, twice for president against Jokowi.

Perhaps seeking to keep him close, Jokowi named Prabowo as Minister of Defense in 2019. But approaching the 2024 elections, Prabowo has now named Jokowi's eldest son, Gibran Rakabuming Raka, as his running mate. Jokowi's son is technically too young to run for the office, but the Constitutional Court, in response to Gibran's possible interest in becoming vice president, added a timely exception to the requirements for running for vice president to allow people under 40 years of age who had already held "national positions" to seek the office.

Gibran has been the Mayor of Solo, the same position that launched his father's political career, since 2020.

So Indonesian national politics are showing their clear return to dynastic intergenerational control at the highest levels, with the same being true in several provincial governments as well. As a result, there is little of actual consequence at stake in the upcoming elections; the choice is merely between which celebrity-style candidate will represent which party. The real client at hand is the continued power of the political and business elites, most of whom will be represented in the government no matter who wins. But Widodo's willingness to have his son skip political parties to run with Prabowo, who is the candidate of the *Golkar* movement that is still quite alive even following the fall of Suharto, signals that Indonesian politics is much less of a lively democracy than the Reformation of 1998 aspired to. The upcoming presidential elections in 2024 are, therefore, according to Yosef Djakababa "frustrating, and increasingly we are seeing and confirming our long fear that Jokowi may become the new Suharto."

Foreign policy across Indonesian history

Indonesia's foreign policy strategy since achieving independence in 1949 has been to hold a non-aligned, or (as Indonesians referred to it) a "non-bloc," position in world affairs. But this should not be confused with a passive role. Indeed, President Sukarno was central to planning the first international conference of the non-aligned movement, the Asia-Africa Conference, which was held in the Indonesian city of Bandung in 1955.

Indonesia's goals for the conference were two-fold. First, Sukarno sought to establish himself and Indonesia as leaders in the emerging post-colonial non-aligned movement, with a particular aim of being one of the movement's principal thinkers and communicators. Second, Indonesians hoped to "open a door from Indonesia to the world," making great efforts to present Indonesian culture and its rich and complex cultural history, a symbol of the nation's political legitimacy, to the visiting delegates and the world's press. These two goals remained at the center of Indonesian diplomatic outreach for the following decade.

At the outset of the Cold War, Indonesia maintained that it was not under the control of either side. Rather, Indonesia would develop relations both sides of the fissure. And while Sukarno's foreign policy veered toward the People's Republic of China in the early 1960s, the idea of non-alignment was only broken after the overthrow of the Sukarno government following the events of September 1965–March 1966.

Throughout its history, Indonesia's political energy has largely been internally focused. National building, whether under Sukarno's USDEK or Suharto's project of Development (*"Pembangunan"*), have taken precedence over global representation. This is not to say that international prestige does not play an important role in the Indonesian concept of the nation; the Indonesian press is quick to focus on Indonesian delegations abroad, often highlighting the national pride that comes from international appreciation of Indonesian culture.

Since its inception in the late 1940s, Indonesian foreign policy has positioned the nation as a buffer and bridge between others. Above all, Indonesia seeks a pliant stability in regional and global systems: good for business, good for profits, good for development. They stress respect for national sovereignty, both their own and that of other nations, and though Indonesian policy also speaks clearly to the need to uphold human rights, Indonesian diplomats rarely press these issues at the expense of regional harmony, and when they do so, they often express Indonesia's positions obliquely.

Ahmad Rizky M. Umar, an Indonesian political scientist, refers to this as part of a growing "rise of Asian middle powers," in which Indonesia's conception of international order is "premised on a desire to pursue autonomy in international politics." Drawn originally from the "*Bandung* philosophy" of Indonesia's first vice president, Mohammed Hatta, Umar notes that the desire to position Indonesia in the "middle" was reasserted after the fall of the Suharto regime in 1998 by President Susilo Bambang Yudhoyono and President Joko Widodo. Each took slightly different approaches, he notes: "On the one hand, Yudhoyono sought to 'perform' Indonesia's identity in the liberal international order as a home-grown democracy. Widodo, on the other hand, has been highlighting how material impacts of the liberal integration order can deliver equitable development." Widodo's approach has been particularly visible in his moves to control the nickel market, but also in how he has approached Indonesia's relationship with China.

As it has across the global South, China has brought its belt and road initiative to Indonesia, both investing in large-scale infrastructural projects (the latest was the construction of Southeast Asia's first high-speed railway line between Jakarta and Bandung, which opened in October 2023,) and in economic projects such as the nickel smelting facilities allowing Indonesia to flex its political muscles within the global economy. But Indonesia remains wary of China's intentions around industrial scale marine fishing in its waters, and of China's expressions of practical control of the South China Sea. But, as it often does, Indonesia threads a middle ground on these issues, as it does between questions of American-Australian and Chinese influence on foreign policy, while maintaining the importance of Indonesian national sovereignty within a Southeast Asian regional context.

This was highlighted in coverage of ASEAN's first ever joint military exercises, held in September 2023 in Indonesian waters during current mounting tensions between China and the United States over Chinese claims of control over 90% of the South China Sea. Commenting on the nature of the exercises, which centered primarily on developing skills in maritime security, running patrols in national waters, and providing disaster and humanitarian relief, Yudo Margono noted to journalists that the exercises were "not a combat operation because ASEAN is more focused on economics. The training is more about social activities" among the troops from all ten ASEAN members.

This overall approach to Indonesian foreign policy was fully on display at the recent United Nations General Assembly in September 2023. Indonesian Foreign Minister Retno Marsudi opened her speech to the body in what might seem to be an unusual way. "Today I am wearing a traditional fabric from East Nusa Tenggara, Indonesia, while my delegations are wearing different traditional fabrics." This represents, she continued, "the diversity of over one thousand ethnicities in Indonesia. We are diverse, but we are one."

Marsudi went on to distill Indonesia's current diplomatic approach into three clear points: first, that nations should work together collectively to forge a "collective global leadership," so that the "fate of the world cannot be defined by the mighty few;" second, that the global system provide "development for all," in which "every country has the same right to develop and grow," but that currently, "the global architecture...only benefits the selected few;" and third, that Indonesia would reinforce regional cooperation within ASEAN, not allowing Southeast Asia to become "a pawn of rivalries."

Each of these general points connects to specific current Indonesian priorities, though the most important goals that brushed up against more powerful nation's interests—keeping Indonesia clear of the growing pressures to choose sides in American-Chinese tensions in the South China Sea, and defending Indonesia's actions to assert control in the nickel market—were referred to only obliquely. Technology transfer, including for artificial intelligence, was mentioned specifically, but under the general assertion that "industrial down-streaming must not be an exclusive call of developing countries."

Marsudi mentioned two more spe-

Indonesian Foreign Minister Retno Marsudi speaks at the General Assembly during the 10th Emergency Special Session at the 39th plenary meeting at United Nations Headquarters on October 26, 2023, in New York City. EDUARDO MUNOZ ALVAREZ/GETTY IMAGES

cific political objectives. Both involved rights of self-determination and human rights, an interesting development for Indonesian diplomacy. The first objective is a long-held position: support for a Palestinian state, a tenet of Indonesian foreign policy since 1950, from which Indonesian would not "back [down] an inch." Second, Marsudi called for support for Afghan women's rights, including the right to education. The call emerges from Indonesia's long-held commitments to women's fundamental equality in society, including within Islamic contxts.

Finally, Marsudi addressed ongoing human rights violations and crackdowns in Myanmar. Marsudi deferred to ASEAN's timid "five point consensus" that the Burmese junta has agreed to, but has not implemented. The reliance on toothless agreements to handle internal issues within ASEAN states remains the Indonesian approach. But the consensus was developed in a summit in Jakarta and under Indonesian leadership with Singapore and Malaysia in 2021, and this point's single-sentence inclusion in the speech was as much about reasserting Indonesia's established role in regional leadership as it was about conditions in Myanmar.

Marsudi's address to the UN was anodyne, and perhaps even milquetoast. Gently reasserting its role as a regional leader, quietly mentioning one or two elements it might claim some small international space in, and reconnecting Indonesia in international eyes both to its rich, varied culture now unified as "Indonesian" as a symbol of home-grown democracy and to its history at Bandung as a leader of the Global South that is following a middle road. It was a speech in which nothing much happened, and which seems to be almost empty of any important meaning.

But Marsudi's speech was also tightly calibrated to Indonesia's conception of itself and its place in the world. There was not a single sentence, not even her introduction of her staff sporting regional fabric, that did not specifically reflect Indonesia's complex history of building national identity and policy, or stake out, even if obliquely, Indonesia's intended role in Southeast Asia's economic and political future. But for Americans to capture those subtle meanings, we must be aware of these subtleties and be able to reflect them back, sometimes equally quietly, to Indonesians, demonstrating we understand what they are doing, and why, and that, hopefully in the end, our mutual relationship can be less frustrating.

INVISIBLE INDONESIA

Discussion questions

1. As Indonesia threads the needle between U.S. and Chinese plays for influence in Southeast Asia, what elements of Indonesian foreign policy and leadership in ASEAN seem to be particularly important in the current day?

2. Is present-day Indonesia a democracy? The relationship between political leadership and average Indonesians has at times been authoritarian and controlling, despite the presence of elections. As Indonesia approaches new presidential elections in 2024, what can we read about the democratic elements of these elections from Indonesia's past?

3. Indonesia has had to fight for control of its own economy since the colonial era. Dutch policies created a tightly governed plantation system for things like spices, coffee, indigo, and later rubber and oil, which were largely processed to their final forms outside the archipelago. This remained true to an important extent in the New Order as well, particularly around palm oil, minerals, and petroleum, and Indonesian factory labor worked for multi-national corporations like Nike. Within this history, how might we contextualize President Widodo's current international positions about Indonesia's nickel industry?

4. Famously, Barack Obama grew up as a young boy in Jakarta, attending Indonesian schools. One criticism of him as a president was that he was reserved and quiet, rather than authoritative. How might Obama's history as a "third culture kid," particularly one who grew up in Indonesia and then Hawaii, have affected both his own leadership styles, and how his critics have perceived him?

5. Clothing makes the man, so the saying goes, or in this case the woman. To open her UN General Assembly speech in 2023, Indonesian Foreign Minister Marsudi noted that she and her staff were wearing fabrics from across the archipelago, a symbol of Indonesian unity and democracy. It is highly unlikely, however, that her UN staff came from all the places represented by their clothing. How might clothing, and particularly modern styles based in "traditional" fabric designs, serve as an example of Indonesians becoming "one people?" and how is Minister Marsudi's use of clothing here more than simply a discussion of fashion?

Suggested readings

Melvin, Jess, **The Army and the Indonesian Massacre: Mechanics of Mass Murder.** London: Routledge, 2018. One day while doing archival research in Aceh, Jess Melvin was handed an army document from October 2023, showing the military's immediate reaction to the events in Jakarta earlier that day. Something like this had never been seen by historians before as the New Order had tightly controlled the documentary evidence of its own establishment by violence. This slim and powerful, carefully written book has changed forever the history of modern Indonesia.

Mrázek, Rudolf, **Engineers of Happy Land, Technology and Nationalism in a Colony.** Princeton, NJ: Princeton University Press, 2002. An intellectual tour-de-force, Mrázek uses lenses of technologies of multiple sorts: roads, clothing, lighting, radio and language, to explore the interactions of modernity and nationalism in the development of Indonesia during the late Dutch colonial era. Along the way, in the words of Harvard University's Mary Margaret Steedly, by "considering technology and the ways that people use and think about *things*, Mrázek invents an original way to talk about freedom, colonialism, nationalism, literature, revolution and human nature." So quite the read, whether about Indonesia or the human experience in the early 20th century in general.

Pemberton, John, **On the Subject of "Java."** Ithaca, NY: Cornell University Press, 1994. One of the finest works of colonial anthropology ever written, Pemberton's deep research in both the archives of Central Javanese court culture and ethnographically in late New Order Indonesia allows him to make fascinating connections between the power structures of social control built into both Dutch colonialism and Suharto's New Order.

Pisani, Elizabeth, **Indonesia Etc.: Exploring the Improbable Nation.** New York, NY: W.W. Norton and Company, 2014. On its surface a "travel" book, Pisani's exploration of Indonesia's improbable unity from stories at local levels reflects her long experience in Indonesia as both a journalist and an HIV epidemiologist. Exceptionally accessible and engrossing.

Ricklefs, M.C., **A History of Modern Indonesia since c. 1200.** Stanford, CA: Stanford University Press, Fourth Edition, 2008. For those looking for a good "general history" of Indonesia, Ricklefs' graduate school standard is the choice. Detailed but not stuck in the weeds, this work balances the need to be comprehensive with being readable and incredibly well structured.

Don't forget to vote!

Download a copy of the ballot questions from the Resources page at www.fpa.org/great_decisions

---

To access web links to these readings, as well as links to additional, shorter readings and suggested web sites,

GO TO **www.fpa.org/great_decisions**

and click on the topic under Resources, on the right-hand side of the page.

7
The High Seas Treaty

A humpback whale jumping on August 29, 2006, off Madagascar, Mozambique Channel, Indian Ocean. Despite weighing 40 tons, humpback whales can jump and sometimes propel themselves almost entirely out of the water. ALEXIS ROSENFELD/GETTY IMAGES

On June 19, 2023, the 193 member states of the United Nations adopted an international legally binding marine biodiversity agreement following nearly two decades of heated negotiations, This agreement is the first single international instrument to address biodiversity on the high seas as a whole and is commonly referred to as the Biodiversity Beyond National Jurisdiction (BBNJ) agreement or the High Seas Treaty. It is a legally binding instrument under the 1982 UN Convention on the Law of the Sea (UNCLOS) and is intended to ensure conservation and sustainable use of marine biodiversity in areas beyond national jurisdiction. It will enter into force 120 days after the 60th nation ratifies it. But where did this journey begin?

This GREAT DECISIONS chapter includes two sections: one discusses the state of the oceans and the role of the Law of the Sea and the second describes the new High Seas Treaty.

The first section is excerpted from a GREAT DECISIONS article from 2012 written by Sara Tjossem entitled "State of the oceans: waves of change." The second part is reprinted with permission of the American Society of International Law from their Insights publication. It was written by Cymie R. Payne.

7 State of the oceans

For many air travelers, crossing the ocean is measured in interminable hours of unremitting blue flatness. Perhaps a flash of light or twist of wave might punctuate this boredom with thoughts of whales or other deep-sea creatures. Over a century ago the American writer Henry David Thoreau observed, "The ocean is a wilderness reaching round the globe, wilder than a Bengal jungle, and fuller of monsters...." Indeed, the ocean's aerial monotony masks a remarkable diversity of form, function and use. Although one can speak of a single ocean of salt water, its regional variation is hinted at by names such as the Atlantic, Pacific, Indian, Arctic and Southern Ocean, along with a multitude of smaller seas. The global ocean plays an integral role in climate and weather, supports at least half of all species, and provides about a quarter of the animal protein in the human diet. A billion people count on seafood for their primary source of protein, while countless towns and cities rely on the economic engine of fisheries to provide direct employment to some 200 million people. The global economy is predicated on cargo ships that move almost all internationally traded goods.

Despite the ocean covering over two thirds of the world's surface, humans have explored less than 5% of it. Generations of people thought and acted as though it was so vast as to be beyond human influence, an inexhaustible source of fish and adventure. The most recent scientific consensus, however, suggests that the ocean is highly vulnerable to cumulative human action, including fishing, resource extraction and pollution—effects that are exacerbated by climate change. An increasing number of citizens and policymakers fear that the rapidly deteriorating conditions of the oceans will profoundly reduce human welfare. Advocates for a holistic, unified marine policy warn of imminent global marine collapse, especially as climate change magnifies other long-standing threats. The global reach of oceans has made international maritime governance both critical and difficult to achieve. In order to understand what options exist for future ocean governance, it is necessary to assess the shift in mankind's relationship with the oceans and in turn, the implications for current resource management and governance initiatives underway around the world. Only renewed public attention to the vital role of the oceans will lead to their lasting future.

Growing scientific and popular understanding

Although the oceans have provided fish and access to new lands since prehistoric times, scientific exploration began only in the mid-19th century. Matthew Fontaine Maury—dubbed "Pathfinder of the Seas" for having developed a uniform method for recording currents and winds—published the first extensive book on oceanography in the 1850s. The 1870s voyage of the HMS Challenger produced the first systematic scientific explorations of the biological, physical and chemical marine environment. Its scientific results required 50 volumes that took almost a quarter century to compile, and only touched upon the vast complexity of the oceans.

Scientific accounts were matched by an outpouring of popular stories to excite the layperson through a mix of adventure, science and natural history storytelling that built upon Americans' fascination with the myth of the Wild West. Some of these stories were pure scientific adventure, while others began to question what they saw as the arrogance of man's exploitation of the seas. By the 1950s, the biologist and writer Rachel Carson introduced a new generation of readers to the unfolding mysteries of the seas with her trilogy portraying ocean life from its shores to its surface and finally to its profound depths. Her love of the sea led her to question the wisdom of the exploitation of its riches before understanding the full consequences for the future of both ocean and mankind. The adventures of French marine biologist Jacques Cousteau and his crew brought the wonders of the deep into even more homes and inspired a new generation of marine adventurers and scientists. Popular and scientific research interest throughout the 1960s and 1970s helped a broad audience see the ocean as a wonderous frontier rather than a watery "desert."

In fact, at the 1964–65 New York World's Fair, the General Motors (GM) Futurama exhibit envisioned that "mankind can make great future strides in every area of the globe if it exercises its full potential." The wild frontier of ocean exploration and exploitation promised such a future. In prose conjured up by GM's styling staff, the publicity brochure explained: "Three quarters of our earth lies beneath the cold still deeps of the sea. A water world in which we now can find abundance far beyond our dreams. Now we can farm and harvest a drifting, swimming, never ending nourishment; food enough to feed seven times the population of the earth. In aquacopters search the ocean floor to find, miles deep, vast fields of precious minerals and ores. And in the deepest trenches of the seas, study at first hand long hidden secrets of survival. Work easily the rich oil deposits of the continental shelves while trains of submarines transport materials and goods along the waterways of the under sea."

How have these aspirations been realized in the modern world, with a global population that has just exceeded eight billion people? An increase and intensification of ocean use, compounded by the development of new

---

! Before you read, download the companion **Glossary** that includes definitions, a guide to acronyms and abbreviations used in the article, and other material. Go to **www.fpa.org/great_decisions** and select a topic in the Resources section. (Top right)

HIGH SEAS TREATY

types of coastal and ocean activities, has led to increased user conflicts and loss of functional habitats. It is now known that the ocean plays a vital role in the global climate system, absorbing carbon dioxide (CO2) from the atmosphere and producing oxygen. Increasing levels of greenhouse gases are bringing about changes in the ocean as rising sea levels and acidification are putting both marine ecosystems and coastal communities at risk. Effective ocean policy and management plans must take into account past and current uses and mitigate their impacts.

At the international level, the United Nations has been the forum where nations and intergovernmental organizations develop and monitor plans for the variety of regional and local initiatives for management inside their national jurisdictions.

Early resource management

Because the ocean is vital to national security and economic vitality, it has spawned both conflict and cooperation. International and local policy initiatives must grapple with an apparent "tragedy of the commons" condition, further complicated by the interaction between international governance—or collective action—and the protection of state sovereignty.

Perhaps the most instructive example of conflict and attempted cooperation on the seas is the management of ceivable that open-sea fish stocks were vulnerable. The British scientist Thomas Henry Huxley famously held that the great sea fishes must be inexhaustible so it was unreasonable and unfair to try to regulate poor fishermen.

At first when a fishery failed, it was natural enough to suggest that the fish had moved elsewhere, or that ocean conditions had turned unfavorable, but the collapse of more and more fisheries prompted increased efforts at regulation. The number of bilateral and multilateral fisheries treaties proliferated over time as managing different species required different approaches. By the 1900s in Europe, growing concern over the condition of fish stocks in the North Sea combined with developing marine re-

KITTISUN KITTAYACHAROENPONG/GETTY IMAGES

LL28/GETTY IMAGES

The photo at left shows a school of long-nosed emperor fish at Richelieu Phangnga, Thailand. The photo at right is a green turtle, Chelonia mydas, at a cleaning station in Maui, Hawaii, USA. The green turtle is a large, weighty sea turtle with a wide, smooth carapace, or shell. It inhabits tropical and subtropical coastal waters around the world and has been observed clambering onto land to sunbathe.

usage and conservation of the global ocean commons beyond the limits of national jurisdiction. Its efforts to bring order and stability to "the common heritage of mankind" produced a constitution for the seas, the UN Convention on the Law of the Sea (UNCLOS). Along with protection of navigation rights and coastal state authority over offshore resources, one of the driving motivations for a treaty was the prospect of commercial seabed mining. Meanwhile, governments and nongovernmental organizations (NGOs) had developed a living marine resources. Marine fish populations are notoriously difficult to assess because they can move from near shore to open ocean without regard for artificial political boundaries. Coastal and open ocean management influence each other in complex ways. Informal fisheries management has existed for hundreds of years, while formal, government-based attempts only started in the last century. Concern about fish stocks grew in Victorian times, as some near-shore fisheries were overfished, but it seemed inconsearch produced the first international marine scientific organization in the world: the International Council for the Exploration of the Sea (ICES), which still produces and supports cutting-edge marine research and provides advice on fisheries management to its member nations and the 28 members of the European Union (EU). An analogous regional organization, the North Pacific Marine Science Organization (PICES), now promotes and coordinates research for the far North Pacific, though without a fisheries management component.

73

Creating a law of the sea

After World War II, efforts got underway to reach an international agreement on the use of ocean resources. The 17th-century principle of "freedom of the seas" limited national rights and jurisdiction to a narrow coastal strip, while the remainder of the seas was free to all. The oceans proved to be an early canvas for international policies on access to fisheries, ocean dumping and pollution, and oil and gas rights.

By the 20th century, rapid technological advancements had opened new ways to exploit offshore resources, with offshore oil production moving to increasingly deeper waters and long-distance fishing fleets harvesting unprecedented tons of fish, while transport ships and oil tankers increased the hazards of pollution. In an effort to decrease conflict over competing claims, the UN General Assembly (UNGA) resolved to create a common law of the sea that would determine the limits of coastal state authority and promote greater use and better management of ocean resources in both territorial and high seas. (See box on next page.)

The first attempt to codify international law for the seas failed to determine a new breadth for territorial waters, but ensured the principle of freedom of fishing, which encouraged the development of long-distance industrialized fishing fleets. In 1954 the British stern freezer trawler *Fairtry* introduced to the Grand Banks off Newfoundland a new era of large vessels equipped with the latest technology for unprecedented hauls of fish. Seven years later the first Soviet vessels appeared there, quickly growing to a fleet of over 100 ships. The post-World War II (WWII) development of such factory ships that could stay for months at sea with new, more powerful equipment to find and harvest fish signaled an intensified level of efficiency and destruction as both targeted and "incidental" fish were caught. When fisheries collapsed, people saw a classic example of a tragedy of the commons; too many boats chasing too few fish.

After an inconclusive second conference in 1960, the third UN Conference on the Law of the Sea (UNCLOS III, 1973–82) labored for nine years to write a comprehensive treaty for the oceans that would address the contentious issues of resources, sovereignty and superpower rivalry. In the meantime, the U.S. enacted the Magnuson-Stevens Act in 1976, which established eight regional councils made up of commercial and sport fishers along with agency staff to manage stocks. Their overarching goal was to achieve optimal yields from fisheries while restoring depleted stocks, with the right to determine how many fish could be caught, by whom and with what gear. They had good success at rebuilding stocks where regulations were faithfully enforced, but that was difficult and expensive to do. The political pressure to maintain the livelihoods of fishing communities and the fishing industry could overwhelm conservation ideals. In 2011 the National Marine Fisheries Service reported to Congress that of the 197 stocks monitored for overfishing, 39% of them were subject to overfishing or clearly overfished.

UNCLOS III finally came into force in 1994. A veritable "constitution for the ocean," it provides a legal framework within which all legal ocean activities must operate, defining maritime zones, such as the 200-mile EEZ that gives coastal states exclusive rights to manage and share living and nonliving ocean resources in this space while ensuring freedom of scientific research. That management provision required that nations protect stocks from overexploitation and that they either harvest their entire allowable catch or give access to the "surplus" to other countries, an arrangement that some scientists have argued fosters mandated overfishing.

Competing uses for ocean resources

Humans have long used the ocean to provide food, energy, transportation and waste disposal while weaving it into social and cultural life. The most recent excitement has been over the potential for energy and food generation, including possible offshore wind farms up and down the north- and mid- Atlantic coast, and fish farms off the coast of Chile. As technology allows new and greater exploitation of the ocean's resources, ongoing challenges surrounding jurisdictions, governance and sustainability—in addition to the will to implement and execute any policy decisions—will continue to confront policymakers around the world

Mining and drilling

In the 1970s, the eccentric billionaire Howard Hughes was credited with fostering excitement over the potential riches of manganese nodules plucked from the ocean floor, though his ship, the Hughes Glomar Explorer, was never meant for that use (it was used for the secret retrieval of a sunken Soviet submarine). Other attempts in the 1970s and early 1980s to mine the sea floor for manganese nodules did not result in commercial operations since growth in demand slowed as new land-based sources came on line, but they nevertheless produced both interest and the techniques for later exploration of other geologic formations like hydrothermal vents. The first underwater geyser was discovered in 1977 by oceanographers, and was seen as a geological curiosity. It is now known that vents influence ocean chemistry, temperature and circulation, and play host to unique species of tubeworms, clams, shrimp and bacteria. Since these first observations, commercial firms have intensified their search for vents with the realization that vents accrete dense and pure mineral deposits on their flanks in potentially commercial amounts. The particularly harsh conditions of low light and oxygen combined with extreme temperatures may also provide building blocks for new industrial processes and products derived from this bacterial action, similar

Evolution of the 'law of the sea'

After WWII, advances in technology for offshore oil development and ocean fishing led to national claims over marine resources and territory beyond the traditional three-mile territorial sea. With the Truman Declaration in 1945, the U.S. led the way by announcing a unilateral right to resources on its continental shelf. Other states soon followed, claiming fisheries zones of 4 to 200 miles. These competing claims posed a serious threat to military and civilian freedom of navigation, open seas fishing and other maritime activities.

In the early 1950s, the International Law Commission, established by the UNGA in 1948, attempted to promote the codification of these new claims into international law. In 1958, four conventions were produced, addressing the territorial sea, fisheries, the continental shelf and the high seas. The conventions defined rights and duties, but failed to reach agreement on the outer boundaries of national authority over territorial waters, fisheries or the ocean floor. A second conference in 1960 was unable to resolve these same issues.

In the 1960s a new approach was taken: instead of negotiating separate treaties, the goal was a comprehensive convention on the ocean that could address the essential security interests of all nations and accommodate their most important economic, environmental and scientific concerns. Championed by the U.S. and the then-U.S.S.R., the goal was also to obtain universal ratification of the convention in order to manage future ocean issues through a peaceful process involving all nations.

After years of painstaking negotiations, UNCLOS was completed in 1982. It achieved almost all of the ambitious objectives set for it. It provided protection for navigational freedoms while establishing a 200-mile exclusive economic zone (EEZ) in which coastal states managed all economic development; developed a new set of provisions governing the marine environment and scientific research; and created a regime to manage the exploitation of minerals of the seafloor beyond the limits of national jurisdiction.

It was this last issue—deep seabed minerals—however, that derailed the final agreement. The Reagan Administration (1981–89) conducted a thorough review of the draft convention as it stood in early 1981. The U.S. review found the regime for deep seabed minerals—which had been negotiated during the turmoil of decolonization and ideological disputes between developing countries and the industrialized world—to be unacceptable. Before the final negotiations began, Reagan laid out six criteria, all related to the seabed minerals regime, that were necessary in order to make the convention acceptable to the U.S. In the final version, these criteria were not met, so the U.S. opposed the adoption of the convention and pressured its allies not to sign it. President Reagan did declare in 1983 that the U.S. would abide by all parts of UNCLOS except for the deep seabed mining provisions.

In 1990, as the number of ratifications slowly rose toward the 60 needed to bring the convention into force, developing states and industrialized allies prevailed on the U.S. to seek a modification of UNCLOS that would meet all six of Reagan's criteria. This effort proved successful, and in 1994 the Agreement Relating to the Implementation of Part XI of the UN Convention on the Law of the Sea that modified the implementation of the seabed provisions along with the rest of the convention was signed by President Bill Clinton. The Agreement and the Convention were then sent to the U.S. Senate for its advice and consent, where both have languished ever since, despite strong support from every President and Cabinet, all of the Navy and Coast Guard leadership, heads of shipping, energy, fishing and telecommunications industries, and the environment and conservation community. However, partisan politics and other business deemed more pressing than the oceans have prevented the convention from being debated by the full Senate.

---

to what has occurred in better known terrestrial hot springs.

Advances in marine geology and deep ocean technology have opened up depths previously unattainable. In the past few years, deep-sea mining firms from Canada, Australia, Russia and China have intensified their interest in exploiting copper, gold, silver, lead and zinc in deepwater areas around the world, often off small island nations like Papua New Guinea. In some cases, the deep-sea robotics now used by the offshore oil and gas industry has prompted mining interests to see water as an easier barrier to overcome than an equivalent amount of rock. That access comes with drawbacks, however. Hydraulic pumping increases nutrients in deepwater areas and potentially produces harmful algal blooms, while the sediments stirred up will certainly interfere with or kill filter-feeding organisms that are a critical component of marine ecosystems. More than land-based mining, these pollutants are likely to spread via currents through large areas of water. All this economic interest in mining the sea floor has raised concern among small island nations, legal experts, scientists and environmentalists about the ecosystem effects because there are few international standards and safeguards. The island nations with jurisdiction over rich deposits have neither guidelines nor sufficient information to balance environmental interests against the potential income from selling mineral concessions.

The New High Seas Biodiversity Treaty Offers Conservation, Equity, and Regulatory Certainty

Oxygen production, food, carbon dioxide sequestration, and more than ten million species of living creatures (some of surpassing beauty) are found in the marine environment beyond national jurisdiction, which encompasses nearly half of the Earth's surface. Its intrinsic value and our dependence on the ecosystem services it provides are sufficient reasons to protect it, yet less than one percent is now protected under international law. This ocean space shared by all nations is inhabited by life forms that are able to thrive under crushing pressure, intense heat and cold, total lack of sunlight, and the chemical outpourings of hydrothermal vents. Their adaptations are mapped in their genetic codes, called marine genetic resources (MGR). Products based on this information have already been commercialized for uses that include medical treatments and food crops, but the regulatory framework is uncertain, and benefits primarily flow to states with advanced technology.[1] Better governance for conservation, a more certain regulatory situation for investment, and integration of equity can now become a reality with the new High Seas Biodiversity Treaty.

The Treaty was adopted on June 19, 2023, as the third implementing agreement to the UN Convention on the Law of the Sea (UNCLOS).[2] This new international agreement seeks to fulfill UNCLOS's objectives to protect and preserve the marine environment in areas beyond national jurisdiction (ABNJ) (the seabed, the water column, and, by inference, the air space above), to ensure adequate assessment and monitoring of potentially harmful activities, to acknowledge the shared ocean as the common heritage of humankind, to promote the transfer of marine technology on fair and reasonable terms and conditions, and to support the development and use of marine scientific research.[3]

In this era of struggle between nationalism and multilateralism, the treaty represents a commitment to solve global problems together, with most states parties to UNCLOS and several states that have not ratified UNCLOS participating in the negotiation. The adoption of the treaty text by consensus reflected their enthusiasm. This Insight details its underlying approach, describes the history leading up to the Treaty, outlines its major features, and identifies some outstanding questions about its relationship to UNCLOS.

The Treaty's Approach to Marine Conservation and Its History

The Treaty's biodiversity conservation measures seek to prevent injury to ocean life and to build its resilience to harms that cannot be prevented. Humanity faces a triple planetary crisis: biodiversity loss, climate change, and pollution. Therefore, the Treaty's central strategies to conserve marine biodiversity are to prevent or reduce damage from activities that humans can control by requiring environmental impact assessment of new and unregulated activities in ABNJ and to limit activities in marine areas characterized by values like uniqueness, rarity, and vulnerability to ocean warming and acidification.

As early as 2000, civil society organizations like the International Union for Conservation of Nature called for the international community to protect ocean life. In 2004 the United Nations created an ad hoc open-ended informal working group to study issues relating to the conservation and sustainable use of marine biological diversity beyond areas of national jurisdiction (BBNJ). Completing the task would take another 19 years.[4] The BBNJ Working Group

At left, plastic Waste washed up at Greta Beach, Christmas Island, Australia. At right, scavengers collect valuable waste at Sidoarjo garbage dump in East Java, on June 5, 2018. About eight million tonnes of plastic waste are dumped into the world's oceans every year—the equivalent of one garbage truck of plastic being tipped into the sea every minute... of every day. Over half comes from five Asian countries: China, Indonesia, the Philippines, Thailand and Vietnam, according to a 2015 study in Science journal.

HIGH SEAS TREATY

Worldwide Exclusive Economic Zone and High Seas

An "Exclusive Economic Zone," or "EEZ" is an area of the ocean, generally extending 200 nautical miles (230 miles) beyond a nation's territorial sea, within which a coastal nation has jurisdiction over both living and nonliving resources. The high seas lie beyond the EEZ.

■ EXCLUSIVE ECONOMIC ZONE

LUCIDITY INFORMATION DESIGN, LLC

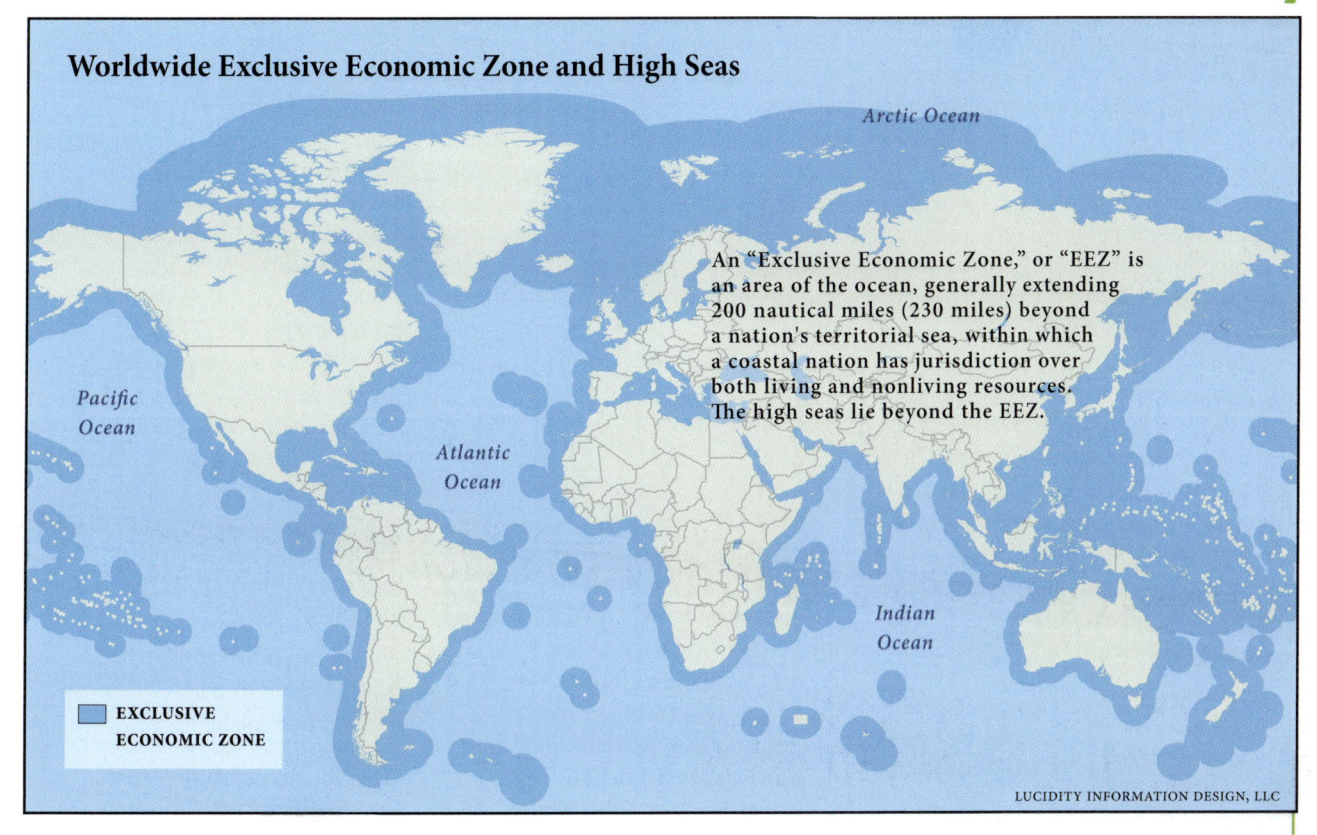

fashioned the 2011 "package deal" addressing four elements, discussed below. The 2012 UN Conference on Sustainable Development called for a new implementing agreement under UNCLOS, advancing step by step toward the negotiation of a treaty.5

In 2015 the UN General Assembly launched the negotiation of the High Seas Biodiversity Treaty, which came to be known as the "BBNJ Agreement"6 and has the formal title "Agreement under the United Nations Convention on the Law of the Sea on the conservation and sustainable use of marine biological diversity of areas beyond national jurisdiction." The 2015 resolution established a Preparatory Committee tasked with developing the basic treaty elements. Two years later, the UN General Assembly further mandated the negotiation of the BBNJ Agreement.7 Seven meetings were held over the next several years, with interruption and delay caused by Covid.

The final negotiating session continued through the night of March 3, 2023, and into the following evening, when an agreed text was welcomed by the exhausted delegates with the declaration by the President of the intergovernmental conference, Ambassador Rena Lee, that "the ship has reached the shore." The High Seas Biodiversity Treaty will be opened for signature on September 20, 2023, at the United Nations, and will remain so for two years. Entry into force will require 60 states to accept, approve or ratify it. Supporters of the treaty are urging states to sign and to ratify so that it comes into force by 2025.

The Package Deal and Institutions

The UN General Assembly mandated four parts to the Treaty, based on the package deal:

the conservation and sustainable use of marine biological diversity of areas beyond national jurisdiction, in particular, together and as a whole, [1] marine genetic resources, including questions on the sharing of benefits, [2] measures such as area-based management tools, including marine protected areas, [3] environmental impact assessments and [4] capacity-building and the transfer of marine technology.8

It included the proviso that "the process indicated in paragraph 1 above [i.e., the negotiation] should not undermine existing relevant legal instruments and frameworks and relevant global, regional and sectoral bodies."

Potentially the most consequential result of the Treaty will be the creation of the Conference of the Parties (COP). UNCLOS does not provide a regular forum for states to meet, set policy goals, and collaborate to achieve them, although we are used to seeing the climate change regime and other multilateral agreements make good use of their COPs. Other treaty bodies will include a Scientific and Technical Body, a Secretariat, and a Clearing-House Mechanism. Committees are also established for access and benefit-sharing, capacity-building and transfer of marine technology, finance, and implementation and compliance.

General principles and approaches set out in Article 7 capture principles found in UNCLOS and reflect more recent developments in international environmental law. An element shared with UNCLOS is the non-transfer of damage or hazards from one area to another and the non-transformation of one type of pollution into another.9 The polluter pays principle reinforces the statement in the Preamble that "as set out in the Convention, States are responsible for the fulfilment of their international obligations concerning the protection and preservation of the marine environment and may be liable in accordance with international law." Formulations of precaution were intensely debated, with divergent views ultimately reconciled by reference to "the precautionary principle or precautionary approach, as appropriate."

Common Heritage, Freedom of the High Seas, and Marine Genetic Resources

Is the ocean beyond national jurisdiction a commons belonging to all humanity? Hard-fought agreement was reached to include "the principle of the common heritage of humankind which is set out in the Convention." In the final hours, this wording was accepted along with reference to "the freedom of marine scientific research, together with other freedoms of the high seas." The addition of the two letters "hu" to the UNCLOS "common heritage of mankind" brought important gender equity, a revision that was heartily welcomed by delegates when it was proposed. "The principle of equity and the fair and equitable sharing of benefits," also in the principles section, is a corollary to the common heritage.

These principles are fundamental to the question of who can take ownership of high seas resources, whether that means fish or the information embedded in the genetic code of diverse ocean life. UNCLOS, Article 87, asserts the freedom of fishing in the high seas, but it does not mention MGR. The new Treaty treats MGR as a shared resource, and the developed/developing state asymmetry of access and ability to develop actual or potential value from MGR and digital sequence information is addressed in the Treaty through the sharing of non-monetary and monetary benefits.10 The Clearing-House Mechanism is the site where notices of activities from sample collection to commercialization are published, and it also may be used to access relevant traditional knowledge held by Indigenous Peoples and local communities with free, prior, and informed consent.

Area-Based Management Tools, Including Marine Protected Areas

The COP may establish area-based management tools, including marine protected areas (Part III)11 to create a connected network of high seas marine protected areas through a state-led procedure. A state or a group of states may submit a proposal for a marine protected area or other measures that limit or coordinate specific activities. The proposal must include identification of the area to be protected, the threats it faces, and a draft management plan. During a consultation process, stakeholders will have an opportunity to review and comment on the proposal, and the proponents will be able to revise the proposal based on the input they receive. The Treaty's Scientific and Technical Body then will review and assess the proposal and will provide a recommendation to the COP. The COP will decide whether or not to establish the marine protected area. The text also

provides guidelines for implementation, monitoring, and review of the marine protected areas that are established.

Environmental Impact Assessment

The environmental impact assessment (EIA) provisions 12 build on the general international law obligation to conduct EIAs and provisions found in UNCLOS; they also allow for the eventual development and use of strategic environmental assessment. The provisions require that states parties conduct environmental impact assessments for unregulated and new activities in areas beyond national jurisdiction. Assessments prepared under other legal regimes must be reported through the Clearing-House Mechanism. Principles of transparency and access to information by stakeholders are reflected in the requirements for public notification and consultation that begin with scoping potential impacts of a planned activity and continue through the review process. The state party with jurisdiction or control of the planned activity may decide whether to proceed with an activity when "the Party has determined that it has made all reasonable efforts to ensure that the activity can be conducted in a manner consistent with the prevention of significant adverse impacts on the marine environment," and taking into account mitigation or management measures proposed to limit harms from the activity.13 The state must then monitor the impacts of an authorized activity under its jurisdiction or control in accordance with the conditions set out in the approval of the activity. If significant adverse impacts are observed, the state must notify the COP and the public and take measures to address the harm.

Capacity Building and Transfer of Marine Technology

An essential component for developing states, capacity is referenced throughout the Treaty and in a dedicated section.14 The objectives are to provide what is needed for developing states to implement the Treaty, to participate in its activities, and to develop scientific and technical capacity in relevant fields. While UNCLOS states similar commitments, they have not been fully implemented, so the modalities included in this Treaty attempt to apply lessons learned for a more successful outcome.

Relationship to UNCLOS

It has been a matter of debate whether or not the Treaty is an implementing agreement to UNCLOS. Implementing agreements are intended to operationalize principles and general measures stated in the parent treaty, and relevant parts of the parent treaty generally carry through to the implementing agreement. Some argue that this Treaty goes beyond UNCLOS by integrating concepts from international environmental law. Alternatively, the evolution of law under UNCLOS through the BBNJ Agreement can be understood as part of the same process also observed in the climate change and ozone regimes that respond to new knowledge and policy needs. Moreover, in Article 197, UNCLOS itself calls on states to cooperate in developing rules "for the protection and preservation of the marine environment."

A different basis for arguing that the Treaty should not be considered an UNCLOS implementing agreement is that a number of states that were very active in the negotiation are not parties to UNCLOS, including the United States, Colombia, Turkey, and Venezuela. For them, it was important to establish the non-application of parts of UNCLOS that they do not already consider themselves bound by as customary international law. Accommodations were made in the text for their concerns, in Article 5(3), stating that non-parties' legal status is not affected by the Treaty, and in Article 60, Procedures for the settlement of disputes. The dispute settlement measures in UNCLOS, Part XV, will apply to UNCLOS state parties, while those provisions "shall be deemed to be replicated" for disputes involving non-UNCLOS parties. In electing a means of dispute settlement, non-UNCLOS parties may choose the International Tribunal for the Law of the Sea, the International Court of Justice, or either of the two different arbitral tribunals described in UNCLOS; UNCLOS parties make their election of these alternatives under UNCLOS. Further specific measures are included to address situations such as the existence of dispute settlement mechanisms provided by another "relevant legal instrument or framework" and disputes that might involve maritime boundaries between a coastal state and areas beyond national jurisdiction subject to the Treaty. Should disputes arise under this Treaty, the jurisdictional issues may prove complex to parse.

It will now be for the UN General Assembly to authorize a Preparatory Commission in advance of the Treaty's entry into force, to request the UN Office of Legal Counsel's Division of Ocean and Legal Affairs to support that work, and to make arrangements for financial support so that developing states are able to participate fully.

A humpback whale in New Zealand's Cook Strait, June 27, 2007. Perched high on a clifftop overlooking the stretch of sea dividing New Zealand's South and North Islands, four former New Zealand whalers keep watch on the whales as they joined the conservation cause in helping New Zealand's Department of Conservation in a survey of humpback whales migrating north through New Zealand's Cook Strait The hunters are now protectors but the instincts of the former whalers are as sharp as ever as they scan the wild waters of New Zealand's Cook Strait. DAVID BROOKS/AFP/ GETTY IMAGES

HIGH SEAS TREATY

Discussion questions

1. What are the strategic considerations that should be incorporated into U.S. ocean policy? What is the role of the ocean in the global economy? Where does the ocean fit into the national security and counterterror agenda? How does the ocean affect U.S. relations with its neighbors? How does the ocean figure into food security?

2. Do you think that the High Seas Treaty will be more successful than past agreements on the environment? Why or why not? How would you define success—countries ratifying the treaty? Seeing an impact on the state of the oceans?

3. In the last few years, effects of climate change, such as wild fires, and floods, have made people more aware of how time is running out on "fixing" climate issues. Will this attitude make the BBNJ agreement more likely to be ratified?

4. The United States has signed but not acceded to the Law of the Sea Treaty (UNCLOS) and recognizes it as codification of existing international law. Do you think the U.S. will ratify the High Seas Treaty? Would doing so be detrimental to economic or foreign policy interests?

5. How much of an impact do you think climate change has on biodiversity loss? Is pollution more or less of a factor in your opinion?

6. What impact do you think fishing has on the oceans and biodiversity? Will countries with large fishing fleets that operate on the high seas be willing to curtail the size of their catches? Why or why not?

Suggested readings

Kurlansky, Mark, **Cod: A biography of the Fish that Changed the World.** New York, Penguin, 1998. In this accessible volume, Kurlansky traces cod's prominent rold in history from the Viking exploration of North America to the depleted fisheries of today.

Marlow, Jeffrey, "The Inside Story of the UN High Seas Treaty," **The New Yorker,** March 9, 2023. https://www.newyorker.com/news/daily-comment/the-inside-story-of-the-un-high-seas-treaty

Patrick, Stewart, "The High Seas Treaty Is and Extraordinary Diplomatic Achievement." Carnegie Endowment for International Peace, Commentary, March 8, 2023. https://carnegieendowment.org/2023/03/08/high-seas-treaty-is-extraordinary-diplomatic-achievement-pub-89228

"Ten Things You Should Know About the High Seas Treaty," https://www.nature.org/en-us/what-we-do/our-insights/perspectives/ten-things-high-seas-treaty/

"What we know about the new High Seas Treaty," **Nature,** https://www.nature.com/articles/s44183-023-00012-x

Don't forget to vote!
Download a copy of the ballot questions from the Resources page at www.fpa.org/great_decisions

To access web links to these readings, as well as links to additional, shorter readings and suggested web sites,
GO TO **www.fpa.org/great_decisions**
and click on the topic under Resources, on the right-hand side of the page.

Pandemic preparedness
the deadly cycle of panic and neglect
by Carolyn Reynolds

WHO Director-General Tedros Adhanom Ghebreyesus (Far L) and Mayor of Geneva Marie Barbey-Chappuis attend the opening of a photo exhibition entitled "Picturing Health" to celebrate the World Health Organization's 75th anniversary in Geneva, on April 6, 2023.
FABRICE COFFRINI/AFP/GETTY IMAGES

March 11, 2020: Along with December 7, 1941, and September 11, 2001, it was a day when America and the world changed. World Health Organization (WHO) Director-General Tedros Adhanom Ghebreyesus announced to the world that the novel and fast-spreading coronavirus Covid-19 was indeed a pandemic. Over the next 48 hours, the White House and other governments declared a state of emergency. Stock markets plunged, offices shut down, schools closed, extracurricular activities and social plans were canceled, and stores were mobbed as people raced to stock up on food and cleaning supplies. Like many others, I sat my family down and told them I did not know what was going to happen, but that we should prepare to stay at home and for our lives to be disrupted for the foreseeable future. Little did we know just how much disruption was to come, or for how long.

The global fallout of Covid-19

It would be more than three years later, on May 5, 2023, before Dr. Tedros declared that Covid-19, while still a pandemic, would no longer be considered a public health emergency of international concern (PHEIC)—the highest formal designation of an infectious disease outbreak under international law (to note, a pandemic is currently a political declaration by the Director-General with no universally adopted

CAROLYN REYNOLDS *is co-founder of Pandemic Action Network whose mission is to drive global action to prevent the next pandemic. She is also a non-resident fellow with the Center for Strategic and International Studies and adviser to the Bipartisan Alliance for Global Health Security. She has held senior roles at PATH, World Bank Group, and U.S. Global Leadership Coalition. She holds a Master of International Affairs from Columbia University and B.A. from the University of Virginia.*

...tions, although it is widely understood to be a global epidemic). The combined human, economic, and social toll of Covid-19 has been simply staggering. As of October 18, 2023, almost seven million lives had been lost globally according to official death counts reported to WHO, with some experts estimating the actual number to be multitudes higher—24 million—based on available excess mortality data. The United States accounted for the largest number of deaths worldwide by far at 1,136,920, more than twice the number of Americans killed in World War II, the Korean War, and the Vietnam War combined. New variants, cases, and deaths continue to emerge, and Covid-19 poses an ongoing health risk. Life expectancy declined globally; in 2020–21, the U.S. saw the largest two-year decline in more than a century, exacerbating racial and other inequities. The severe secondary health impacts of the pandemic—from mental health and heightened risks for cancer and cardiovascular disease patients to extensive disruptions in HIV/AIDS treatment, childhood vaccinations, and other preventative care—are well-documented and continue to pose risks to human health around the world.

Economic fallout

The Covid-19 pandemic triggered much more than a global health crisis. It was accompanied by historic drops in output in almost all economies and is conservatively estimated to have cost the global economy at least $16 trillion in emergency response and fiscal stimulus packages, as well as incalculable losses in jobs and livelihoods as businesses shuttered or pivoted to virtual work and economies underwent a structural shift. By some estimates, by the end of 2025, the pandemic will have cost the world $28 trillion. It has also resulted in a stunning and historic reversal of global progress in learning, gender equality, and the Sustainable Development Goals, including the largest one-year increase in poverty reduction in at least two decades, along with a debt "tsunami" in the poorest countries. UNICEF has warned that the scale of learning loss among children worldwide due to school closures during the pandemic is "nearly insurmountable," while the World Bank has called it "one of the mass casualties of Covid-19." As seen with the secondary health impacts of the pandemic—and as is the case with most shocks—vulnerable populations have been hurt the most by these setbacks.

While high-income economies have largely rebounded, for many developing countries, the near-to-medium-term economic outlook remains weak. This has been worsened by the so-called polycrisis—the pandemic combined with the fallout from with the war in Ukraine, climate change-driven natural disasters, global energy and food crises, and persistent high inflation rates (and now, as of this writing, war in the Middle East). In its October 2023 World Economic Outlook, the International Monetary Fund (IMF) found that global economic growth remained sluggish. This presages a potential new health crisis in the making. A July 2023 report by the World Bank found that public health spending has dropped precipitously as the Covid-19 emergency recedes, with 21 out of 78 (roughly one-fourth) of studied countries spending less on public health than 2019 pre-Covid levels, and 37 countries (roughly half) deprioritizing health spending relative to 2019. The World Bank predicts that with contractions in overall government expenditures due to debt and fiscal space constraints, health spending will remain lower in 40 low- and middle-income countries than before Covid-19 until at least 2027, precisely the period when much higher public investments are required to fuel recovery and growth.

There have been some silver linings from the pandemic. Perhaps the greatest story was that of the achievement of medical science, which mobilized with unprecedented speed and focus to produce effective Covid-19 vaccines in record time. Before Covid-19, getting a new vaccine from concept to approval would typically take up to a decade. Yet within weeks of the first case of Covid-19 being reported, researchers had identified the virus they suspected of causing the disease, decoded an initial genome sequence, and made it available to researchers around the world. Thanks to years of prior investment in vaccine platform development—and the successful messenger RNA (mRNA) technology, along with a surge of billions in financing from U.S. Operation Warp Speed and others—the first vaccines were ready to test within two months. With expedited clinical trials and regulatory approvals for emergency use, the first FDA-approved vaccines were administered within 300 days. The pandemic also spawned structural innovations across education, public services, and in almost every industry with rapid uptake of online technologies and telework.

Inequitable response

Sadly, however, the pandemic also exposed the underbelly of humanity. As the new virus and associated panic began to spread in its early weeks and months, governments quickly turned inward and nationalism kicked in. Of course, it is the first responsibility of every government to protect and provide for the welfare of its own people. Yet in the case of a global threat such as a pandemic—where pathogens know no borders and can spread quickly out of control with the ubiquity of global air travel and migration—the lack of strong international leadership, and the failure to adopt a mindset and approach of global solidarity and collective security, paved the way for a prolonged crisis and a highly inequitable response. The United States, Canada, European Union, United Kingdom, and other high-income countries hoarded the available supply of new vaccines, preordering in some cases several times the amount they would need to vaccinate their entire populations, pushing lower-income countries to the back of the queue. By mid-2020, international

---

! Before you read, download the companion **Glossary** that includes definitions, a guide to acronyms and abbreviations used in the article, and other material. Go to **www.fpa.org/great_decisions** and select a topic in the Resources section. (Top right)

PANDEMIC PREPAREDNESS

leaders agreed to set up a global pooled purchasing platform, COVAX, with the goal to provide all countries with equitable vaccine access, but it was already too late to rectify vaccine inequity. As of mid-August 2021, when wealthy (defined as high- and upper-middle-income countries) had reached, on average, 60% of their populations with at least one vaccine dose and had begun donating their excess doses, the average coverage for low-income countries stood at just 1%. Duke University's Launch and Scale Speedometer found that the G7 was likely to have more than 3 billion spare doses that year. By January 1, 2022, when both donations and manufacturing had ramped up, the average vaccination coverage for low-income country populations still stood at less than 10% compared to 77% for wealthy countries. Even as late as July 2023, the vaccination gap remained wide: 31% coverage for low-income countries versus 84% for wealthy countries. This gap is even wider considering booster shots, which remain difficult to obtain in low-resource settings, as do Covid tests and treatments.

The global Covid-19 vaccine inequity is a profound humanitarian and human rights issue. It has also caused serious collateral damage in terms of global policy. From an epidemiological perspective, the emergence of the dangerous omicron variant in southern Africa, which resulted in a global surge in Covid-19 cases and deaths in late 2021 and the first half of 2022, was widely attributed to the delays in global vaccine delivery. As WHO Director-General Tedros warned at the time, "No country can vaccinate its way out of the pandemic alone." The delays also allowed mis- and dis-information about the safety of the vaccines, fueled by a determined and growing group of anti-vaccine activists, to take hold in various populations and parts of the world that previously had been highly motivated to get themselves and their families protected. Donated and even purchased vaccine supplies often arrived in developing countries so late that they were close to their expiration dates and countries had little time to

Worldwide Covid-19 Cases (as of 11-05-23)

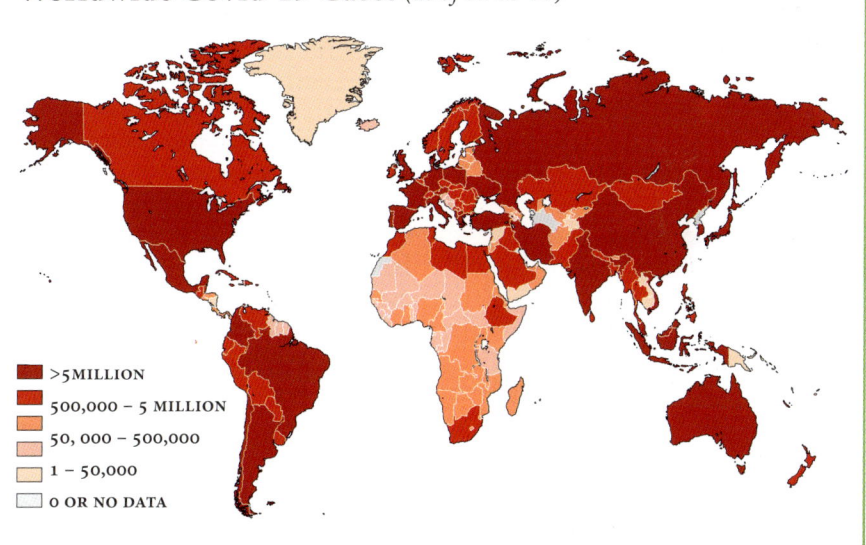

Legend:
- >5 MILLION
- 500,000 – 5 MILLION
- 50,000 – 500,000
- 1 – 50,000
- 0 OR NO DATA

Top Ranked Covid-19 Cases by Country

	TOTAL COVID CASES	TOTAL DEATHS	PERCENT VACCINATED	% RECEIVING A BOOSTER
United States	103,436,829	1,138,309	66.18%	35.23%
China	99,318,718	121,790	87.3%	56.69%
India	45,001,384	533,294	69%	16.58%
France	38,997,490	167,985	78.37%	60.47%
Germany	38,437,756	174,979	76.37%	62.65%
Brazil	37,721,749	704,659	80.66%	51.93%
South Korea	34,571,873	35,934	86.38%	65.62%
Japan	33,803,572	74,694	81.75%	68.47%
Italy	26,257,548	192,554	83.83%	76.09%
United Kingdom	24,804,243	231,324	75.45%	N/A

World Vaccination Rates By Income

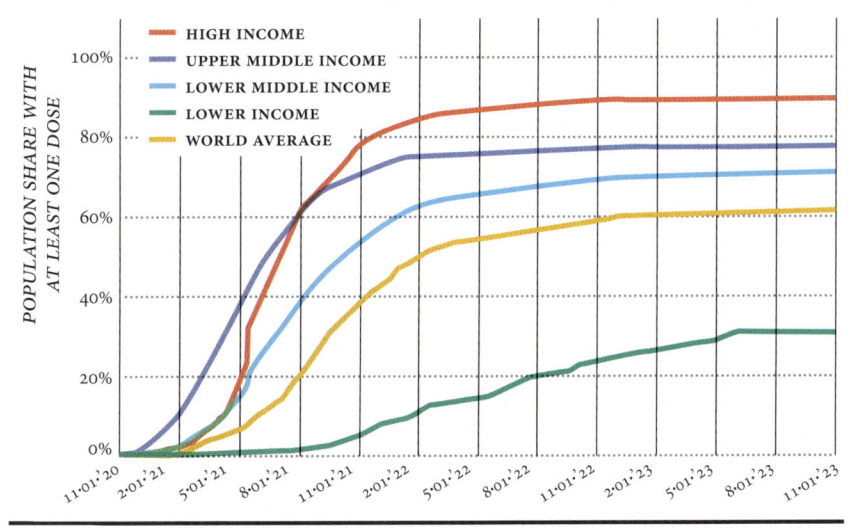

Legend:
- HIGH INCOME
- UPPER MIDDLE INCOME
- LOWER MIDDLE INCOME
- LOWER INCOME
- WORLD AVERAGE

Y-axis: POPULATION SHARE WITH AT LEAST ONE DOSE (0% – 100%)
X-axis: 11-01-'20 to 11-01-'23

SOURCE: WORLD HEALTH ORGANIZATION; KFF NEWS SERVICE   LUCIDITY INFORMATION DESIGN, LLC

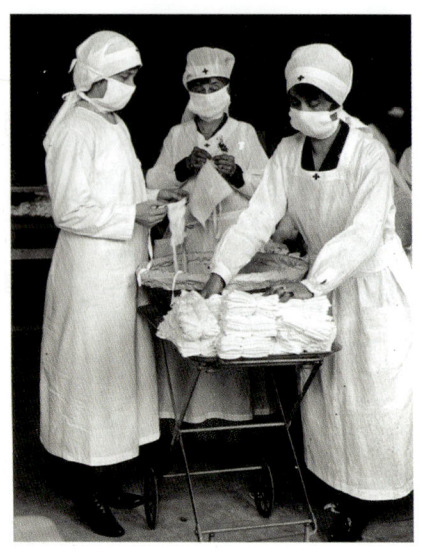

Red Cross workers of Boston, Massachusetts remove bundles of masks designated for American soldiers, while other nurses are busy making them, March 1919. PHOTOQUEST/GETTY IMAGES

prepare mass vaccination campaigns, leading millions of doses to be discarded. In parallel, the wealthiest countries dragged their feet on a proposal introduced in 2020 by India and South Africa at the World Trade Organization (WTO) for member states to adopt a Trade-Related Aspects of Intellectual Property Rights (TRIPs) waiver for Covid-19 vaccines, which would have enabled low- and middle-income countries to ramp up generic production; agreement on a more limited waiver was not reached until much later, in July 2022. (It is noteworthy that the Biden administration came out early in support of the waiver.) This inequity and lack of global solidarity enraged leaders in Africa and across the Global South, who in September 2021 took to the United Nations General Assembly (UNGA)—most speaking virtually, due to the same lack of vaccines—to denounce what Namibia President Hage Geingob called "vaccine apartheid." This resentment and breach of trust has imperiled multilateral cooperation in various fora, as was recently on display at the 2023 UNGA, where developing countries once again found their concerns sidelined and deliberations on even a relatively unambitious, non-binding political declaration on pandemic preparedness, prevention, and response was highly fraught.

With impacts of such magnitude from a crisis that negatively affected every country, every system, and nearly every human on the planet, one would think that political leaders would unite across party and geographical lines to do everything possible to end Covid-19 and prevent another devastating pandemic from happening again. In the very early months of the pandemic, there was a great deal of rhetoric to that effect from national and world leaders. Yet it did not take long for the pandemic to become quickly politicized. In the United States, for example, opposition to issues such as mask and vaccine mandates became political sparring points, and scientific leaders became the targets of withering attacks and even death threats. In mid-2020, President Donald Trump announced that he would commence U.S. withdrawal from WHO over criticism of its engagement with China on the pandemic (a decision later reversed by President Joe Biden when he entered office). The American Rescue Plan Act, President Biden's signature legislative initiative to ramp up the domestic and global Covid-19 response and jumpstart recovery efforts, passed Congress without Republican support, and Congress later refused the President's appeals for additional response funding. The President's Fiscal Year 2023 budget request to Congress, which included an unprecedented, mandatory budget ask of US$88 billion for global and domestic pandemic preparedness and biodefense, was never given serious consideration on the Hill.

By the second half of 2022, with thousands still dying each day from Covid-19, pandemic fatigue had already begun to set in with both the American and global public. In contrast to the 9/11 response, when a U.S. president marshalled the country and the world to unite to combat terrorism, the pandemic response faded as a political priority. With midterm elections looming in the U.S. and the war in Ukraine dominating foreign policy, political leaders saw little upside to pushing for major new investments in pandemic preparedness and response. Once the end of the Covid-19 emergency was declared in spring 2023, pandemic fatigue metastasized into collective pandemic amnesia, with most politicians and their publics eager to put the crisis firmly in the rearview mirror—leaving the world arguably even less prepared than before.

How did we get here?

Human history has been awash with pandemics and major epidemics over the centuries. The first recorded pandemic occurred in Athens during the Peloponnesian War (430 B.C.), possibly killing up to two-thirds of Athens' population. In 1350, the bubonic plague (or "Black Death") was responsible for killing one-third of the world's population. In 1918, the so-called Spanish Flu, propelled by World War I, killed an estimated 50 million people worldwide. More recently, the HIV/AIDS pandemic swept across the United States and rest of the world and continues to this day; more than 70 million people have been infected and 35 million have died to date. Severe Acute Respiratory Syndrome (SARS) was first identified in 2003 and is believed to have possibly started with bats before spreading to humans in China and 26 other countries, infecting more than 8,000 people, causing nearly 800 deaths and an estimated US$40 billion in economic losses. The 2009–10 H1N1 (swine flu) pandemic reached more than 70 countries and is estimated to have killed up to half a million people. The West Africa Ebola outbreak from 2014-16, while not officially declared a pandemic, was highly deadly, infecting more than 28,000 people and killing more than 11,000, an alarming case fatality rate of 40%.

While the overall impact of SARS was relatively contained, its high case fatality rate of nearly 10% gave impetus for the international community to take steps to improve global outbreak response. A major conclusion was that the International Health Regulations

PANDEMIC PREPAREDNESS

(IHRs), which were first adopted by the World Health Assembly in 1969 and later amended in 1973 and 1981, were too narrow to promote early outbreak detection, prevention, and response in the face of a novel pathogen. As amended in 2005, the IHRs serve as a binding agreement among 196 states parties under international law. They were expanded to cover more diseases, create a new class of event, the PHEIC, and lay out new requirements and processes for global outbreak monitoring, reporting, and cooperation. Under the IHRs, states parties are obligated to build and maintain core outbreak preparedness capacities in 13 areas, such as surveillance, biosafety and biosecurity, human resources, laboratories, zoonotic events, chemical and radiation events, health service provision, financing, emergency plans, and more. The changes were also designed to improve the way WHO works with states to investigate and respond to outbreaks.

The IHR (2005) entered in force in 2007. Yet when the H1N1 pandemic struck just two years later, the lack of global readiness persisted. An independent panel of experts set up to assess the international response, led by then-Institute of Medicine president Harvey Fineberg, concluded that despite the new IHRs, "the world is ill-prepared to respond to a severe influenza pandemic or to any similarly global, sustained and threatening public health emergency" and warned that "tens of millions could die if there is a severe flu outbreak in the future." The panel issued a series of recommendations for WHO. Five years after the pandemic, Fineberg reflected that some improvements had been made, namely the adoption of WHO's Pandemic Influenza Preparedness (PIP) Framework, which provides access to flu vaccines in developing countries and the sharing of flu viruses for disease surveillance. Yet he found that other systemic constraints remained: chief among them that IHR compliance was too reliant on countries' own self-assessments. After the crisis faded, so did the urgency for further reform.

The deadly West Africa Ebola outbreak and ensuing panic brought the

A woman washes her hands at the Phebe Hospital in Bong Town, central Liberia, on May 27, 2019, as the health authorities lead a campaign in hand washing due to the Ebola virus crisis in the region. ZOOM DOSSO/AFP/GETTY IMAGES

issue of outbreak preparedness back up on global policymakers' agendas. The global Ebola response was widely criticized as far too slow, with the sharpest criticism directed toward WHO for failing to alert the world sooner, almost nine months after the virus is believed to have first emerged in rural Guinea. Once the media began to broadcast graphic images of desperate people dying, politicians felt the pressure to act. A massive international response was launched, including deployment of the U.S. military and the UN Mission for Ebola Emergency Response (UN-MEER), the first-ever UN emergency health mission, authorized by resolution 69/1 of the General Assembly and 2177 (2014) of the UN Security Council. Billions were committed toward the response and recovery efforts, notably a $5 billion emergency supplemental appropriation from the United States alone, which included $1 billion to strengthen global health security.

Even before the Ebola outbreak had been reported, the Global Health Security Agenda (GHSA) launched by the Obama Administration aimed to build a community of countries to learn from each other's best practices in health security and promote a race to the top in IHR core capacity-building. In the wake of Ebola, more than 70 countries joined the GHSA. The GHSA also gave rise to the global uptake of Joint External Evaluations (JEE), a voluntary exercise in which countries invite external expert teams to assess their core capacities. As an independent, transparent, and multisectoral assessment, the objective of the JEE process is to help countries identify their weaknesses and inform preparedness planning. As of 2019—before the onset of Covid-19—more than 100 countries had undertaken JEEs, and a majority of those had developed National Action Plans for Health Security (NAPHS) in accordance with the IHR Monitoring and Evaluation Framework, yet only a small fraction of these plans were financed.

In the wake of Ebola, more expert panels were convened, and more reports issued, on what went wrong and how to prevent another deadly outbreak. UN Secretary General Ban Ki-Moon convened a high-level panel, which made 27 recommendations for action at national, regional, and global levels. He subsequently appointed a high-level task force to detail and monitor implementation of the recommendations. Beyond the uptake of the JEEs, the Task Force found that the West Africa Ebola crisis had led to some notable improvements in the international health architecture, including the establishment of the WHO Health Emergencies Programme, the Coalition for Epidemic Preparedness

Innovations (CEPI) to advance vaccines against diseases with epidemic and pandemic potential, the Africa Centres for Disease Control and Prevention, and the Pandemic Supply Chain Network, among others. In 2018, the WHO and the World Bank also created the Global Preparedness Monitoring Board (GPMB), comprised of leading experts in global health with a mandate to report regularly on the state of the world's preparedness. In its first report in September 2019—again, before Covid—the GPMB sounded the alarm on the immediate threat of a major respiratory pandemic that would cause many millions of deaths and immense damage to the world economy. Other expert assessments around the same time gave similar warnings. Yet none of these have any official authority to act, and by the time their reports came out, the pandemic threat had already been deprioritized once again by political leaders around the world. The cycle of panic and neglect around pandemics was repeating itself.

How do we prevent the next pandemic?

Shortly after Covid-19 was declared a pandemic, the panic phase returned, along with a chorus of calls for "never again." In May 2020, the World Health Assembly agreed to appoint an Independent Panel on Pandemic Preparedness and Response (IPPPR), co-chaired by two former heads of state, Ellen Johnson Sirleaf of Liberia and Helen Clark of New Zealand, and comprised of a diverse group of prominent former political leaders and health experts. After nine months of intensive consultations with stakeholders around the globe on the lessons from the evolving crisis, in May 2021 the Panel issued its landmark report, *Covid-19: Make it the Last Pandemic*. In parallel, the Group of 20 wealthiest nations (G20) commissioned its own High-Level Independent Panel (HLIP) on Financing the Global Commons for Pandemic Preparedness and Response, co-chaired by three former finance ministers, Larry Summers, Ngozi Okonjo Iweala, and Tharman Shanmugaratnam, whose report *A Global Deal for our Pandemic Age* focused on pandemic financing challenges and solutions. Together with the GPMB's third annual report in September 2021, these three panels arrived at strikingly similar conclusions and recommendations—echoing the messages contained in the many pre-Covid reports that were largely ignored by world leaders about the need to prioritize pandemic preparedness.

In his speech to the 2023 World Health Assembly, WHO chief Dr. Tedros warned member states that "The end of Covid-19 as a global health emergency is not the end of Covid-19 as a global health threat… and the threat of another pathogen emerging with even deadlier potential remains." Covid-19 has been mistakenly characterized by some as a once-in-a-century pandemic, yet recent modeling and evidence show that the spread, frequency, and severity of infectious diseases are increasing. Climate change is making future pandemics more likely and the risk of zoonotic spillover of diseases is heightened due to the increased proximity of animal and human habitats. Changing patterns in rainfall, land use, agriculture, and migration are causing the emergence and adaptation of dangerous pathogens through new transmission pathways. For example, during the summer of 2023, malaria emerged in the southern United States for the first time in decades. Some estimates have placed the annual probability of a pandemic on the scale of Covid-19 in any given year to be between 2.5–3.3%, which translates to a 47–57% chance within the next 25 years. Others, including the White House, have made even starker assessments, asserting that another serious pandemic worse than Covid-19 could occur within the next decade.

Global action

A comparison of the various expert reviews of lessons learned in Covid-19 and in previous global health crises point to broad consensus around the five following areas for global action to ensure the world is better prepared to prevent the next deadly pandemic.

■ **Elevate and sustain political leadership on pandemics at the highest levels**

Pandemics are complex emergencies and collective security threats that require ongoing collaboration and coordination across entire governments, sectors, and geographies. They also require a higher level of leadership above and beyond health ministries and global health institutions. The IPPPR, HLIP, and GPMB reports have all highlighted the imperative of political leadership at the head of state or head of government level as one of the most critical elements for effective PPR. Countries which demonstrated strong, decisive national leadership to implement strict public health measures, such as Australia, New Zealand, Vietnam, and Singapore, fared better in the Covid-19 pandemic. In the first year of the pandemic, the failure of world leaders to unite with resolve against a common threat through existing global governance forums such as the G7, G20, or United Nations created a void that contributed to the resulting nationalism and significant delays in the global response. In 2021–22, when G7 and G20 leaders finally came together to prioritize PPR on their political agendas, some significant actions happened, including the launch of a WHO global disease surveillance facility; two global Covid-19 virtual summits convened by President Biden to scale up delivery of vaccines, tests, and treatments; and pledges toward a creation of a Pandemic Fund at the World Bank (more on this below).

Political leaders take for granted that they need to maintain vigilance and invest in military readiness in peacetime to prepare for the next possible terrorist attack or armed conflict, whenever or wherever it may materialize. They should adopt the same national security mindset when it comes to managing pandemic threats. Pandemic preparedness and response should be hardwired into national and global gov-

PANDEMIC PREPAREDNESS

ernance and accountability systems so that it remains prioritized across political transitions. Every country should have a ready, well-funded, and regularly stress-tested health security action plan with clearly delineated roles and responsibilities, overseen by a government-wide coordinating body residing in the executive. The recent decision by the United States to establish a White House Office of Pandemic Preparedness and Response Policy is a good step. Globally, there is need for a standing high-level council or similar body, ideally at the United Nations, that is responsible for overseeing global pandemic preparedness and prevention efforts, regularly assessing emerging infectious disease threats, and helping ensure an equitable response in the event of another PHEIC. While the WHO is the operational nerve center of a global pandemic response, a standing UN body that commands the attention and power of heads of state and government is also necessary to tackle the political roadblocks to global progress and solidarity around this shared threat. Pandemics will never get the priority they deserve if they are seen as only a health sector threat.

■ **Ensure every country has the capacity to stop outbreaks at their source**

Outbreaks are inevitable, but pandemics are not. The IHRs identify the core capacities that every country should develop and maintain to be able to detect, prevent, and respond to outbreaks at their source. At the heart of preparedness is a resilient primary health care system that can deliver essential health services to the local population and pivot quickly to contain an infectious disease outbreak. Key capacities include a well-equipped frontline health workforce that is trained in infection prevention and control; data and disease surveillance systems; widespread testing; sophisticated laboratories; supply chains for medical products; emergency management systems; and culturally sensitive communications and engagement with affected populations. "One health," an integrated approach to human, animal, and planetary health, is another vital

A mass vaccination center inside Gostiny Dvor, also known as the Old Merchant Court, in Moscow, Russia, on July 10, 2021. A surge of infections fueled by the highly contagious delta variant has forced many regions to impose mandatory vaccination requirements and adopt other measures to pressure people to get the shots. ANDREY RUDAKOV/BLOOMBERG/GETTY IMAGES

component, as two-thirds of known infectious diseases and three-quarters of new or emerging infectious diseases are estimated to be zoonotic in origin. For every health crisis, there are dozens of cases of deadly epidemics and pandemics that did not happen because governments and their partners invested in these core PPR capacities and were able to stop outbreaks from spreading. In 2021 alone, these included a Nipah outbreak in India, a new Ebola outbreak in Guinea, and an influenza outbreak in Brazil.

The 2021 *Global Health Security Index,* an independent benchmarking of health security capacities across 195 countries, found that two years into the Covid-19 pandemic, all countries remained "dangerously unprepared to meet future epidemic and pandemic threats," scoring on average 39.8 out of a possible 100 across six indicators, with most lower-income countries ranking in the bottom half. A particular risk area is that the prolonged Covid-19 pandemic has resulted in widespread health workforce burnout, leading to high numbers of resignations. Global health worker shortages were a concern pre-pandemic, and the crisis has only exacerbated this issue, especially in developing countries. It is particularly acute among women, who make up 70% of the overall health workforce and more than 80% of nurses and midwives globally.

■ **Provide timely, equitable access to lifesaving medical countermeasures and tools**

The failure of the international community to provide timely, universal access to Covid-19 vaccines, tests, treatments, and other lifesaving tools has been subject to extensive review. While science produced new countermeasures at unprecedented speed, this was not as fast as it should and could have been to save millions of lives. The pandemic shone a bright light on several longstanding market and systems failures and fragilities that must be addressed to eliminate barriers to effective research, development (R&D) and delivery of health innovations in low- and middle-income countries. The first is the need to scale and sustain investments in platform technologies that can be readily adapted to infectious disease threats. There are about 260 viruses known today to infect humans from 25 known disease families. Entities such as CEPI are aiming to get a head start on this by developing a library of prototype vaccines for the top viral families with pandemic potential, designing clinical trial protocols, and working with regulatory agencies to streamline the bureaucratic hurdles to expedite approvals. CEPI has set an ambitious, but achievable, 100-day mission for moving vaccines from "labs to jabs." The second is the need to engage end-users, especially in the most vulnerable and low-resource communities, from the very outset in the R&D process, to ensure that products are appropriate or adaptable for all. Some of the leading mRNA Covid vaccines, for example, required consistent freezing or refrigeration through ultra-cold chain capabilities that do not exist in many parts of the developing world. Lighter weight, reusable, and gender-appropriate PPE is another area of need to protect frontline health workers.

A strategic shift is also needed from the current charity-based model to one of global solidarity, based on a shared value that all lives are equal and that lifesaving countermeasures are global public goods. This points to third area for improvement, which is to build up globally distributed R&D capabilities in areas such as advanced laboratories, quality-assured manufacturing facilities, and local supply chains. This is vital to reduce the deadly dependency of poorer nations on a limited number of manufacturers who are mostly based in wealthier countries. The sudden decision by India, one of the world's major vaccine producers, to ban exports of Covid-19 vaccines in April 2021, posed a huge roadblock to global access, particularly for Africa. While not every country needs a full suite of R&D capabilities, every country must have a pathway to secure the tools they need at affordable prices when they need them. Biotechnology companies, governments, international organizations, and other funders should scale up their support for international efforts such as the Medicines Patent Pool and mRNA Technology Transfer Hub to promote voluntary licensing, technology transfer, and pooling of intellectual property to accelerate timely access to affordable, lifesaving medicines in low- and middle-income countries. Greater attention and support must also be given to pave the way for downstream readiness of delivery systems and of populations to receive new innovations. For example, the rise of vaccine hesitancy, the erosion of trust in government and science, rampant mis- and dis-information, and the politicization of Covid vaccines all pose red flags for broad uptake of future innovations.

■ **Strengthen global governance and accountability for pandemic threats**

The global nature of a pandemic requires rules of the road that will govern international cooperation. The Covid-19 pandemic has demonstrated that the existing international rules, the 2005 IHRs—which are legally binding, yet rely on a voluntary monitoring and evaluation framework with self-reporting and assessment—are insufficient to drive compliance and the timely, transparent, global sharing of data, tools, and resources that will keep all countries safe. There is also need for stronger global investigative mechanisms, capacities, and systems to address deliberate and accidental events to identify and address the source of outbreaks.

To help address these gaps, in 2022 WHO member states embarked on two significant processes: proposing amendments to the IHRs and drafting a new pandemic international legal instrument or framework conventions, now referred to as the Pandemic Agreement. (Note: this has also been referred to as the pandemic treaty, but that term has been sidelined and the bar lowered as it is evident the U.S. Senate in this politically divided era will never muster the votes to ratify a full treaty). Both the IHR amendments and the Pandemic Agreement have the potential to promote a faster, better, and more cooperative international response to the next health crisis. If adopted, the IHR amendments could bolster the WHO's health emergency executive and bio-surveillance powers and place more onus on states to build and maintain their core IHR capacities. The draft Agreement has the potential to improve pandemic PPR in several ways, namely to enhance the global standards, obligations, and incentives for how countries surveil outbreaks, cooperate internationally, and share data, tools, and resources in a health emergency to protect everyone.

Together with the proposed IHR amendments, implementation of a robust new international agreement could be the difference between localized outbreaks that are swiftly snuffed out and a fast-moving global crisis that kills tens of millions and shuts down economies. It will only drive change, however, if it includes measures to enable and enforce compliance and accountability. Significantly, and as with other international agreements like the Montreal Protocol on Substances that Deplete the Ozone Layer (and more recently supplemented by the 2015 Paris Accord on Climate Change), the proposed Pandemic Agreement would establish a Conference of Parties (COP) to meet regularly to review progress and hold governments to account. Unfortunately, the accountability provisions in the October 2023 negotiation draft are wanting. A critical missing element is an independent monitoring framework, or shadow reporting, which has been an important factor in driving compliance with other international agreements.

The deadline for completion and adoption of both the IHR amendments and Pandemic Accord is the World Health Assembly in May 2024. Further delay could jettison a landmark global agreement for years, if not another generation. Yet both face significant political hurdles to passage, reflecting both the continuing distrust and divides between the Global North and South resulting from the inequitable Covid-19 response, as well as strong opposition from the pharmaceutical industry and their Western allies to any infringements on intellectual property. Whether a final Pandemic Agreement will be binding or non-binding on states' parties is also in question. In addition, in the negotiation draft the proposed COP would only meet once every three years, hardly conveying the requisite urgency. As happens with the climate change COP, world leaders should meet annually to review progress and drive action.

■ **Scale up investments in pandemic preparedness—and have resources ready to flow in a crisis**

None of these measures will be successful without sufficient financing. In response to the warnings and recommendations of the IPPPR, the HLIP, and a determined coalition of global health security experts and advocates, the G20 decided in 2022 to establish the Pandemic Fund as a dedicated

PANDEMIC PREPAREDNESS

new global facility to mobilize additional, long-term financing to accelerate pandemic preparedness in low- and middle-income countries. Based on analysis by the World Bank, WHO, and others, the target investment for the Pandemic Fund is $10.5 billion annually in new international financing over at least the next five years, making up for decades of underinvestment. While this is a significant sum, it is a tiny fraction of the economic costs of the response to Covid-19 or a future pandemic – or the comparable investments in other global challenges – and is an excellent return on investment. The fact that the Pandemic Fund provides financing on grant terms is particularly attractive to incentivize action by resource-constrained countries.

After just one year of operation, as of October 2023 the Pandemic Fund had secured $2 billion in pledges—a good start, but still a far cry from what is required to address what finance experts have called "a dangerously underfunded" global system for pandemic PPR. Initial country requests for support from the Pandemic Fund's first round of grant-making far exceeded the available funding envelope. World leaders now need to finish what they started. The United States has provided about one-third of the total resources to date, and President Biden should marshal a global coalition of other heads of state and government, philanthropies, and private-sector investors to step up and close the rest of the funding gap in 2024. This, in turn, will generate more political momentum for action on pandemics at every level.

One global fund will not solve all of the world's pandemic financing needs. Each country needs to prioritize pandemic preparedness and response efforts into its annual budgets – and protect those budget lines from cuts no matter which party is in power, as usually happens with defense spending. There should be a separate, dedicated source of global surge financing that can rapidly disburse funds to countries in the event of a pandemic, so that their responses are not delayed by fundraising appeals. Investments by wealthy countries should not only come from overseas development assistance

India's Prime Minister Narendra Modi (L) along with Indian President Droupadi Murmu (C) poses with WHO Director-General Tedros Adhanom Ghebreyesus ahead of gala dinner on the sidelines of G20 summit in New Delhi on September 9, 2023. PIB/AFP

(ODA) accounts, but should also come from domestic health and security budgets, with the understanding that supporting other countries to stop outbreaks is in every nation's national security and economic interest. The private sector should also share in the financing burden, given how much businesses have to lose – and to gain – from pandemics; for example, Covid-19 caused mass disruptions to the tourism and corporate real estate industries, while providing a windfall for the pharmaceutical and biotech industries. Policymakers should seriously explore using other innovative financing schemes such as taxes on financial transactions (as has been done for the HIV/AIDS pandemic), airline flights (to enhance airport security), or debt swaps (to combat climate change). And as world leaders push for reforms to enable international financial institutions such as the World Bank and other multilateral development banks to help them tackle emerging global challenges like climate change, pandemic preparedness must also be a priority for new financing. Whatever the budget source, the bottom line is that new pandemic funding must be truly new—additional to existing global health and development spending—and should not force poor countries to take on more unsustainable debt.

Anything is possible with political will

Fully three years into the Covid-19 pandemic, in September 2023, the UN General Assembly convened its first-ever High-Level Meeting on Pandemic Prevention, Preparedness, and Response. World leaders issued a political declaration that, while historic, lacked the resolve, urgency, and firm commitments to near-term action to prevent the next pandemic from happening. Most heads of state skipped the meeting altogether. It was further evidence of how pandemic amnesia and neglect has become firmly embedded in the political class, even as Covid-19 cases continue to spread and there is widespread consensus among experts that next pandemic is not a question of if, but when. A nationwide poll of American voters conducted in January 2023 showed that they expect their political leaders to do what's necessary to prevent the next pandemic—and that they are willing to invest more of their taxpayer dollars in preparedness. Yet most politicians think in the short-term, so they are unlikely to do much—that is, unless they see the political upside and they feel pressure from their constituents to do so. Advocacy groups like mine, the Pandemic Action Network, are working to change this political calculus, bringing groups across the world together to compel policymakers to act while the scars of Covid-19 are still fresh, and not to wait until there is another crisis and panic resurfaces. With pandemic threats on the rise—and the next one could be much worse—the international community must prioritize pandemic preparedness before it is too late.

PANDEMIC PREPAREDNESS

Discussion questions

1. What does the "cycle of panic and neglect" mean when it comes to pandemics, and why does it keep happening?

2. The Covid-19 pandemic has not triggered the same kind of robust foreign policy responses as other deadly crises like WWII or 9/11. Should it have? Why or why not?

3. Does the United States have an interest and responsibility in helping other countries secure access to lifesaving vaccines, medicines, and medical supplies in the event of a global pandemic? Why or why not?

4. Covid-19 exposed the current limitations of international organizations like the World Health Organization to compel countries to cooperate in the face a global pandemic. As with other international agreements under international law, the Pandemic Agreement now being negotiated by countries seeks to address this by strengthening the global rules of the road for everyone. What is the right balance between promoting global solidarity and protecting national sovereignty?

5. What is the most important investment we can make to help stop infectious disease outbreaks from becoming deadly pandemics?

6. How do we foster a culture that values and prioritizes investments in pandemic preparedness and prevention in the same way that we do a strong defense? What should the United States do differently both at home and abroad?

Suggested readings

Global Preparedness Monitoring Board. **A World at Risk.** Gpmb.org, September 2019. The report outlines the acute risk of a devastating global epidemic or pandemic. Convened by the World Health Organization and the World Bank, the GPMB's first report, published a few months before the Covid-19 pandemic, identified seven urgent priority actions leaders must take to prepare for future health emergencies.

High-Level Independent Panel on Financing the Global Commons. **A Global Deal for Our Pandemic Age.** Pandemic-financing.org, July 2021. Report of international panel of mostly economic and finance experts commissioned by the Group of 20 to identify gaps in the pandemic financing and propose actionable solutions to meet these gaps on a systematic and sustainable basis and optimally leverage resources from the public, private, and multilateral institutions.

Independent Panel for Pandemic Preparedness and Response. **Covid-19: Make it the Last Pandemic.** Theindependentpanel.org, May 2021. Report of panel of international leaders and experts established by the World Health Organization (WHO) Director-General to identify insights and lessons learned from the health response to Covid-19 and previous health emergencies and lay out action needed to ensure countries and global institutions, including specifically WHO, effectively address health threats.

Reynolds, Carolyn. "To Prevent the Next Pandemic, Leaders Should Finish What They Started." Council on Foreign Relations, Think Global Health, thinkglobalhealth.org, September 15, 2023. Discusses the state of play for major international pandemic preparedness efforts in the wake of the Covid-19 emergency, and highlights priorities for world leaders in 2024.

Vora, Neil et al. "Want to Prevent Pandemics? Stop Spillovers." **Nature**, May 12, 2022. Expert commentary summarizing key evidence on the increasing likelihood of spillovers of viruses from animals to humans and steps the world needs to take upstream to prevent this from happening in the first place.

Yong, Ed. "We're Already Barreling Toward the Next Pandemic." **The Atlantic**, September 29, 2021. Insightful analysis by a Pulitzer Prize-winning chronicler of the Covid-19 pandemic, examining the reasons for the repeated panic-neglect cycle in the United States and the warning signs of the next crisis.

Don't forget to vote!
Download a copy of the ballot questions from the Resources page at www.fpa.org/great_decisions

---

To access web links to these readings, as well as links to additional, shorter readings and suggested web sites,
GO TO www.fpa.org/great_decisions
and click on the topic under Resources, on the right-hand side of the page.

GREAT DECISIONS MASTER CLASS

This year's edition of the *Great Decisions* DVD features the *Great Decisions* Master Class format. This format will feature 20-30 minute long lectures on the nine topics from this current issue.

Master class lectures are presented by Jeffrey S. Morton, the Pierrepont Comfort Chair in Political Science at Florida Atlantic University and a Fellow at the Foreign Policy Association. He holds a Ph.D. in International Relations from the University of South Carolina and an M.A. from Rutgers University. Dr. Morton has delivered the *Great Decisions* program to live audiences since 1999.

FOREIGN POLICY ASSOCIATION 1918

Become a Member

For nearly a century, members of the Association have played key roles in government, think tanks, academia and the private sector.

FOREIGN POLICY ASSOCIATION 1918

As an active participant in the FPA's Great Decisions program, we encourage you to join the community today's foreign policy thought leaders.

Member—$250
Benefits:
- Free admission to all Associate events (includes member's family)
- Discounted admission for all other guests to Associate events
- Complimentary GREAT DECISIONS briefing book
- Complimentary issue of FPA's annual *National Opinion Ballot Report*

Visit us online at
www.fpa.org/membership

Make a Donation

Your support helps the FOREIGN POLICY ASSOCIATION's programs dedicated to global affairs education.

Make a fully tax-deductible contribution to FPA's Annual Fund 2020.

To contribute to the Annual Fund 2020 visit us online at **www.fpa.org** or call the Membership Department at

(800) 628-5754 ext. 333

The generosity of donors who contribute $500 or more is acknowledged in FPA's *Annual Report*.

All financial contributions are tax-deductible to the fullest extent of the law under section 501 (c)(3) of the IRS code.

FPA also offers membership at the SPONSOR MEMBER and PATRON MEMBER levels. To learn more, visit us online at www.fpa.org/membership or call (800) 628-5754 ext. 333.

Return this form by mail to: Foreign Policy Association, 551 Fifth Avenue, 30th Floor, New York, N.Y. 10176

ORDER ONLINE: WWW.FPA.ORG/GREAT_DECISIONS

CALL (800) 477-5836

FAX (212) 481-9275

☐ MR. ☐ MRS. ☐ MS. ☐ DR. ☐ PROF.

NAME _____
ADDRESS _____
_____ APT/FLOOR _____
CITY _____ STATE _____ ZIP _____
TEL _____
E-MAIL _____

☐ AMEX ☐ VISA ☐ MC ☐ DISCOVER
☐ CHECK (ENCLOSED)
CHECKS SHOULD BE PAYABLE TO FOREIGN POLICY ASSOCIATION.

CARD NO.

SIGNATURE OF CARDHOLDER **EXP. DATE (MM/YY)**

PRODUCT	QTY	PRICE	COST
GREAT DECISIONS 2024 Briefing Book (FPA31736)		$35	
SPECIAL OFFER TEN PACK SPECIAL GREAT DECISIONS 2024 (FPA31743) *Includes 10% discount		$315	
GREAT DECISIONS MASTER CLASS GD ON DVD 2024 (FPA31737)		$40	
GREAT DECISIONS 2024 TEACHER'S PACKET (1 Briefing Book, 1 Teacher's Guide and 1 DVD (FPA 31739) E-MAIL: (REQUIRED)		$75	
GREAT DECISIONS CLASSROOM-PACKET (1 Teacher's Packet & 30 Briefing Books (FPA31740) E-MAIL: (REQUIRED)		$775	
MEMBERSHIP		$250	
ANNUAL FUND 2024 (ANY AMOUNT)			

SUBTOTAL $
plus S & H* $
TOTAL $

*For details and shipping charges, call FPA's Sales Department at (800) 477-5836.
Orders mailed to FPA without the shipping charge will be held.